An Investment in America's Future

An Investment in America's Future

Only in America
Opportunity Still Knocks

1997 Horatio Alger Awards

HORATIO ALGER ASSOCIATION OF DISTINGUISHED AMERICANS, INC.

99 Canal Center Plaza / Alexandria, Virginia 22314

(703) 684-9444

Table of Contents

Charting the Course: The Next Fifty Years

A half century of service and dedication to simple, time-honored ideals of honesty, hard work, integrity, and opportunity. That is the tradition and the legacy the Horatio Alger Association of Distinguished Americans honors in 1997 as it observes its fiftieth anniversary.

Another fifty years of commitment to recognizing leadership, courage, and integrity and to imparting hope, inspiration, and determination to the generations that will follow. That too is the fundamental goal of this golden anniversary year.

We are celebrating a rich and notable past while simultaneously making a pledge to the future—an oath to the nation, and especially to this country's youth, that the Association will embark on its next half century bearing an unyielding resolve to demonstrate the limitless powers of the human spirit given the freedom and opportunities our America can offer to all people.

A Tradition of Service

While the Association's mission has remained constant over the years, much has changed during the organization's half-century of work in providing outstanding role models and educational opportunities to America's young people. The Association has continuously expanded its efforts on behalf of deserving young adults. For example:

- The Horatio Alger National Scholars program is one of the nation's largest privately-funded sources of college financial aid; scholarships awarded now total in excess of $1 million per year. When the program began in 1984, six students received scholarships; in 1997, more than one hundred talented young people will be granted scholarships.

- Annually, millions of Americans learn about the work of Horatio Alger members and the organization through the nationally televised awards program, aired on the Public Broadcasting System (PBS). In classrooms across the country, even more students and their teachers use the PBS broadcast as a learning tool.

- Each year, more than 100,000 high school students participate in Horatio Alger Youth Seminars at their schools.

- Almost 100 colleges and universities have joined the Association's Collegiate Partnership program to ensure that the Horatio Alger National Scholars can successfully complete their undergraduate degrees.

And in keeping with the Association's primary goal of recognizing the modern-day heroes of American society as outstanding role models for our youth, in this 50th anniversary year, the Association is honoring 11 remarkable individuals whose achievements through perseverance and commitment stand as a beacon of encouragement and inspiration for us all. The 1997 Horatio Alger Awardees are:

- **Carlos H. Cantu**, president and CEO of ServiceMaster, who never let prejudice against his heritage stop him from preparing himself for opportunities and taking advantage of them when they came his way;

- **Mary Higgins Clark**, known to her readers as the Queen of Suspense, who went to work as a teenager to help her widowed mother, only to face the same challenge following her own husband's death not long after the birth of their fifth child;

- **Robert L. Crandall**, chairman and CEO of AMR Corporation/ American Airlines, Inc., who has relied on the values of his strict upbringing to guide him in his innovative leadership of the airlines industry;

- **Michael S. Egan**, chairman and CEO of Alamo Rent a Car, Inc., who, when it became necessary, used the skills he developed as a teenager to manage family needs as well as his family's business to build a company that has revolutionized the car rental industry;

- **Alan "Ace" Greenberg**, chairman of Bear Stearns, who worked his way from a job as a clerk to running one of the largest investment firms on Wall Street;

James R. Moffett
Chairman
Horatio Alger Association

George L. Argyros
President and CEO
Horatio Alger Association

Joseph Neubauer
*1997 Awards and
Activities Chair*

- **John "Jack" Grundhofer**, chairman and CEO of First Bank System, who used lessons learned from mentors to help in his rescue of a failing bank, and to put into perspective two harrowing brushes with death—his own and his daughter's;
- **Jon M. Huntsman**, chairman and CEO of Huntsman Corporation, who left life in a Quonset hut to build the largest privately owned chemical, petrochemical, and packaging concern in the world, and who has donated the largest monetary gift to medical research in history;
- **James Earl Jones**, one of the most gifted actors of our time, who was raised by a Mississippi sharecropper, and who found a way to believe in himself enough to overcome years of tormented silence;
- **Patrick C. Kelly**, chairman and CEO of Physician Sales & Service, Inc., who was raised in an orphanage and who learned a lesson there that he

took with him when establishing his own successful medical supply business;
- **Walter Scott, Jr.**, chairman and president of Peter Kiewit Sons', Inc., who worked his way up from stake chaser to the leader of one of the world's largest construction companies;
- **R. E. "Ted" Turner**, vice chairman of Time Warner, Inc., who learned that nothing is impossible even if everyone around you says it is.

The stories of these outstanding men and women are commemorated in this book. Additionally, the book features the 1997 Horatio Alger Scholars as well as updates on the Anniversary Class Members of 1957, 1967, 1977, and 1987.

As we salute the accomplishments and progress of the Horatio Alger Association in this golden anniversary year, we concurrently are carefully preparing for the *next* fifty years. The results of the recent Board of Directors' strategic planning survey indicated over-

whelming member support for the Association's immediate and future goals—expanding educational opportunities, increasing awareness of programs and services, seeking new private sector and philanthropic partnerships.

With the new century now upon us, the Horatio Alger Association stands ready to build upon its long-standing foundation of leadership and commitment to America's youth. Horatio Alger member Joseph Neubauer, chairman and CEO of ARAMARK Corporation and chairman of the 50th Anniversary Awards Activities, captured the essence of these future directions in saying, "We have to continue to let our young people know that the American Dream is still possible. We live in a global society and the need for a good education has never been greater. Our Association stands at a high point of development, but we will never rest on our laurels. We will continue to reach out, to create opportunities, and to say to our youth—'It is possible.' "

Board of Directors

The Horatio Alger Association is directed by a 40-member Board of Directors. To become chairman emeritus, a member must have served as either president or chairman of the Association for at least three years. Chairmen emeriti hold permanent seats on the Board of Directors.

Chairman
JAMES R. MOFFETT ('90)
Chairman of the Board and CEO
Freeport-McMoRan
Copper & Gold Inc.

President & CEO
GEORGE L. ARGYROS ('93)
Chairman and CEO
Arnel & Affiliates

Executive Vice President
RICHARD L. KNOWLTON ('92)
Chairman
The Hormel Foundation

Vice President
ROBERT H. DEDMAN ('89)
Founder & Chairman
ClubCorp International

Vice President
LEONARD L. FARBER ('85)
Chairman of the Board
Leonard L. Farber
Incorporated

Vice President
TERRY M. GILES ('94)
President
Giles Enterprises

Vice President
THOMAS S. HAGGAI ('80)
Chairman and CEO
IGA, Inc.

Vice President

THOMAS L. HARKEN ('92)
Chairman of the Board & CEO
Tom Harken &
Associates, Inc.

Vice President

H. WAYNE HUIZENGA ('92)
Chairman
Huizenga Holdings, Inc.

Vice President

PETER J. JANNETTA, M.D. ('90)
*Walter E. Dandy Professor
and Chairman*
Dept. of Neurological Surgery
University of Pittsburgh
School of Medicine

Vice President

JOSEPH NEUBAUER ('94)
Chairman and CEO
ARAMARK Corporation

Vice President

JOHN V. ROACH ('90)
*Chairman of the Board
and CEO*
Tandy Corporation

Treasurer & Chairman Emeritus

JOHN W. ROLLINS, SR. ('63)
Chairman and CEO
Rollins Truck Leasing Corp.
Rollins Environmental
Services, Inc.

Chairman Emeritus

W. W. CLEMENTS ('80)
Chairman Emeritus
Dr Pepper Company
Director
Dr Pepper/Seven-Up
Companies, Inc.

Chairman Emeritus

DEAN W. JEFFERS ('75)
*General Chairman and
CEO, Retired*
Nationwide Insurance
Companies

Chairman Emeritus

HARRY A. MERLO ('80)
President
The Merlo Corporation

Chairman Emeritus

CHARLES R. SCOTT ('84)
Chief Executive Officer
The Executive Committee

Chairman Emeritus

R. DAVID THOMAS ('79)
*Founder and Senior
Chairman of the Board*
Wendy's International, Inc.

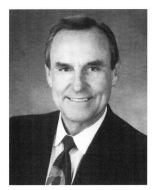

BYRON ALLUMBAUGH ('96)
Chairman of the Board, Retired
Ralphs Grocery Company

DWAYNE O. ANDREAS ('94)
*Chairman of the Board
and Chief Executive*
Archer Daniels Midland
Company

MAYA ANGELOU ('92)
Author/Professor

CARLOS J. ARBOLEYA ('76)
Vice Chairman, Retired
Barnett Bank of
South Florida

JACK H. BROWN ('92)
Chairman, President & CEO
Stater Bros. Markets

ROBERT J. BROWN ('90)
*Founder, Chairman
and President*
B&C Associates, Inc.

S. TRUETT CATHY ('89)
Founder, Chairman & CEO
Chick-fil-A, Inc.

JOE L. DUDLEY, SR. ('95)
President and CEO
Dudley Products, Inc.

WILLIAM F. FARLEY ('86)
Chairman and CEO
Fruit of the Loom, Inc.

RUTH FERTEL ('95)
*Founder and
Chairman of the Board*
Ruth's Chris Steak House

J. B. FUQUA ('84)
Chairman of the Board
The Fuqua Companies

DONALD R. KEOUGH ('88)
Chairman
Allen & Company, Inc.

MELVYN N. KLEIN ('96)
President and
Chief Executive Officer
JAKK Holding Corporation
Managing General Partner
GKH Partners, L.P.

ED McMAHON ('84)
Founder
McMahon
Communications, Inc.

JIM MORAN ('96)
Founder
Chairman of the Board
JM Family Enterprises, Inc.

JOHN PAPPAJOHN ('95)
President
Equity Dynamics, Inc.

ROBERT H. SCHULLER ('89)
Founder & Senior Pastor
Crystal Cathedral Ministries

ROBERT G. SCHWARTZ ('94)
Chairman, President
and CEO, Retired
Metropolitan Life
Insurance Company

HENRY B. TIPPIE ('96)
Chairman of the
Executive Committee and
Vice Chairman of the Board
Rollins Truck
Leasing Corporation

HAROLD TOPPEL ('66)
Chairman Emeritus
Pueblo International

VENITA VANCASPEL HARRIS ('82)
Founder & CEO
VanCaspel & Co., Inc.
Author, Television
Personality, Speaker

DENNIS R. WASHINGTON ('95)
Chairman
Washington Corporations

Founder's Club

M embers of the Founder's Club pledge to contribute to the Association's scholarship fund $20,000 each year over the next five years for a total of $100,000.

GEORGE L. ARGYROS ('93)
Chairman and CEO
Arnel & Affiliates

RICHARD M. DEVOS ('96)
Co-Founder & Former President
Amway Corporation

JOE L. DUDLEY, SR. ('95)
President and CEO
Dudley Products, Inc.

GORDON E. MOORE ('96)
Chairman of the Board
Intel Corporation

JIM MORAN ('96)
Founder & Chairman of the Board
JM Family Enterprises, Inc.

JOHN PAPPAJOHN ('95)
President
Equity Dynamics, Inc.

JOHN W. ROLLINS, SR. ('63)
Chairman and CEO
Rollins Truck Leasing Corp.
and Rollins Environmental
Services, Inc.

HENRY B. TIPPIE ('96)
Chairman of the
Executive Committee and
Vice Chairman of the Board
Rollins Truck Leasing Corporation

DENNIS R. WASHINGTON ('95)
Chairman
Washington Corporations

10

Chairman's Club

Members of the Chairman's Club pledge to contribute to the Association's scholarship fund $10,000 each year over the next five years for a total of $50,000.

BYRON ALLUMBAUGH ('96)
Chairman of the Board, Retired
Ralphs Grocery Company

DWAYNE O. ANDREAS ('94)
*Chairman of the Board and
Chief Executive*
Archer Daniels Midland Co.

HERBERT F. BOECKMANN, II ('95)
Owner/President
Galpin Motors, Inc.

SHEPARD BROAD ('79)
Chairman, Retired
American Savings &
Loan Association

JACK H. BROWN ('92)
*Chairman, President
& CEO*
Stater Bros. Markets

ROBERT J. BROWN ('90)
*Founder, Chairman,
and President*
B&C Associates, Inc.

DEAN L. BUNTROCK ('96)
*Chairman of the Board &
Chief Executive Officer*
WMX Technologies, Inc.

EARLE M. CHILES
President
The Chiles Foundation

JAMES L. CLAYTON, SR. ('91)
Chairman & CEO
Clayton Homes, Inc.

W. W. "FOOTS" CLEMENTS ('80)
Chairman Emeritus
Dr Pepper Company
Director
Dr Pepper/Seven-Up Companies, Inc.

JOHN W. DAVIS ('90)
Chairman of the Board, Retired
Dr Pepper Bottling
Companies of Virginia

JERRY E. DEMPSEY ('95)
Chairman and CEO
PPG Industries, Inc.

LEONARD L. FARBER ('85)
Chairman of the Board
Leonard L. Farber Incorporated

WILLIAM F. FARLEY ('86)
Chairman and CEO
Fruit of the Loom, Inc.

RUTH FERTEL ('95)
Founder and
Chairman of the Board
Ruth's Chris Steak House

JOHN E. FISHER ('93)
General Chairman, Retired
Nationwide Insurance
Enterprise

J. B. FUQUA ('84)
Chairman of the Board
The Fuqua Companies

TERRY M. GILES ('94)
President
Giles Enterprises

JACK M. GILL
Founder and General Partner
Vanguard Venture Partners

HARRY J. GRAY ('84)
Managing General Partner
Investment Fund,
Harry Gray, Mel Klein & Partners, L.P.
Principal, Harry Gray Associates

THE HANSEN FOUNDATION
In Memory of
Zenon Hansen*, a 1974
Horatio Alger Awardee

(*) *Deceased*

THOMAS L. HARKEN ('92)
Chairman of the Board & CEO
Tom Harken & Associates, Inc.

H. WAYNE HUIZENGA ('92)
Chairman
Huizenga Holdings, Inc.

DEAN JEFFERS ('75)
General Chairman and CEO, Retired
Nationwide Insurance Companies

PATRICK C. KELLY ('97)
Chairman & CEO
Physician Sales &
Service, Inc.

DONALD R. KEOUGH ('88)
Chairman
Allen & Company
Incorporated

MELVYN N. KLEIN ('96)
President and Chief Executive Officer
JAKK Holding Corporation
Managing General Partner
GKH Partners, L.P.

RICHARD L. KNOWLTON ('92)
Chairman
The Hormel Foundation

BERNARD MARCUS ('93)
*Founder, Chairman and
Chief Executive Officer*
The Home Depot

ANDREW J. McKENNA ('93)
Chairman, President & CEO
Schwarz Paper Company

LOUIS W. MENK ('78)
Chairman
Black Mountain Gas Co.

JOSEPH NEUBAUER ('94)
Chairman and CEO
ARAMARK Corporation

ALLEN H. NEUHARTH ('75)
Chairman
The Freedom Forum

LOUISE HERRINGTON ORNELAS ('96)
Co-Founder
TCA Cable, Inc.

(*) Deceased

13

D. B. REINHART* FAMILY FOUNDATION
in Memory of
D. B. Reinhart, a 1989
Horatio Alger Awardee

FRANK RESNIK*
Given by Elizabeth Resnik
in Memory of
Frank Resnik, a 1988
Horatio Alger Awardee

JOHN V. ROACH ('90)
Chairman of the Board & CEO
Tandy Corporation

ALBERT A. ROBIN ('91)
Founder
The Robin Construction
Company

O. WAYNE ROLLINS* FOUNDATION
In Memory of
O. Wayne Rollins, a 1986
Horatio Alger Awardee

ROBERT H. SCHULLER ('89)
Founder & Senior Pastor
Crystal Cathedral Ministries

ROBERT G. SCHWARTZ ('94)
*Chairman, President and
CEO, Retired*
Metropolitan Life
Insurance Company

DEEN DAY SMITH ('93)
Chairman of the Board
Cecil B. Day
Investment Company

**JACK D. AND FREDDA S.
SPARKS FOUNDATION**
In Memory of
Jack D. Sparks*, a 1985
Horatio Alger Awardee

R. DAVID THOMAS ('79)
*Founder and Senior
Chairman of the Board*
Wendy's International, Inc.

HAROLD TOPPEL ('66)
Chairman Emeritus
Pueblo International

MONROE E. TROUT ('95)
Chairman Emeritus
American Healthcare Systems

VENITA VANCASPEL HARRIS ('82)
Founder and CEO
VanCaspel & Co., Inc.

(*) Deceased

Specialized Programs

Grants and scholarships are awarded by programs administered by the Association to outstanding secondary school students based on specialized selection criteria.

MARY KAY ASH
Sponsor of the Mary Kay Ash
Foundation National Scholars Program

HARRY A. MERLO
Sponsor of the Harry A. Merlo
Foundation Scholarship Program

LOUIS FEINSTEIN
PUBLIC SERVICE AWARDS PROGRAM
Presented in memory of Louis Feinstein

JAMES R. MOFFETT
Sponsor of the James R. Moffett
Special Assistance Scholarships

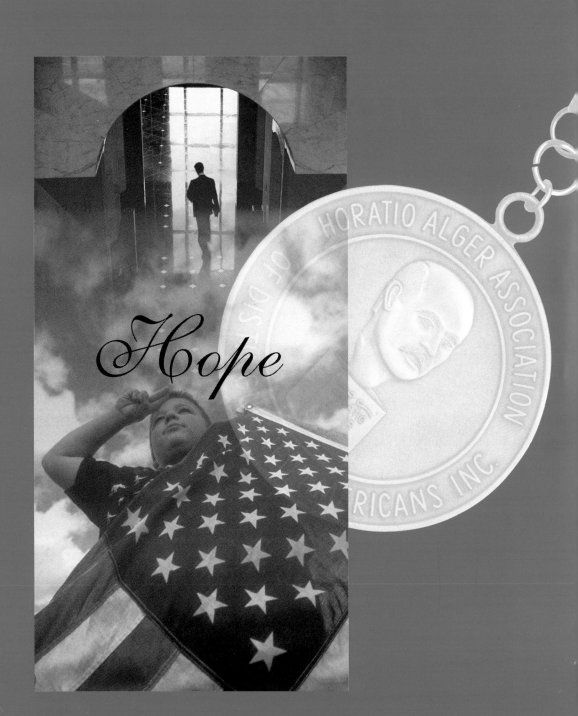

Hope

1997 Horatio Alger Awardees

Carlos H. Cantu

Mary Higgins Clark

Robert L. Crandall

Michael S. Egan

Alan "Ace" Greenberg

John "Jack" Grundhofer

Jon M. Huntsman

James Earl Jones

Patrick C. Kelly

Walter Scott, Jr.

R. E. "Ted" Turner

Carlos H. Cantu

PRESIDENT AND CEO
SERVICEMASTER

Carlos Cantu's father often told him, "Opportunity comes to those who seek it and are prepared for it." Looking for opportunities in the early 1900s is what brought Cantu's grandparents to the United States from Mexico. "My father," says Cantu, "was always searching for a better life for himself and his family. He and my mother were committed to giving their children every chance at succeeding. Later, when big opportunities came my way, I found I was prepared for them. For that, I am indebted to my father and mother and the lessons they taught me."

Hard work was always a part of life for Carlos Cantu's father, Ambrosio. He had to leave school in the third grade when his father, a sharecropper, died. He worked as a child, helping to support his family. Carlos was the first of four children born to Ambrosio and Natalia Cantu.

The Cantu family led a humble life in Brownsville, Texas, but one full of love and encouragement. Both parents were committed to their children and their education. Ambrosio Cantu worked as an auto parts salesman for the Ford dealership in Brownsville, and it was a struggle for him to pay tuition for his children to attend parochial schools. "Education," says Cantu, "was critical in our household. My father and mother knew that it was the only way to reap a brighter future."

Cantu attended a parochial school where English was not emphasized. When he transferred to St. Joseph's Academy in the fourth grade, which was run by the Marist Brothers, he was forced to learn English as quickly as possible. "Many of the brothers at St. Joseph's were from Mexico," explains Cantu, "and they understood that to be productive, competitive citizens in the community we had to be able to speak proper English." An adept student, Cantu moved to the head of his class as soon as he was proficient in English, and stayed at the top throughout his school years.

In addition to understanding the value of education, Cantu's parents instilled in their children a commitment to service and helping others in need. Cantu remembers that in their low-income neighborhood, the Cantu's were the first family to have a telephone. His father had a second job at night running a wrecker service for the dealership. In order for the police to call him when there was an accident, the dealership installed a phone in the Cantu home. As soon as their neighbors learned there was a phone nearby, they lined up to use it. "Not once," says Cantu, "did my parents turn their neighbors away or complain about them using our phone. That was one of my first lessons in realizing that we all have a responsibility to our community."

Embracing diversity is another value passed down to Cantu from his parents. "Mexican Americans in those days," says Cantu, "experienced some racial discrimination. I remember once as a child reading an ad in the newspaper that said, 'Only Anglos need apply.' When I asked my mother what that meant she explained it really meant they were looking for people who could com-

municate. She turned a negative situation into something positive. My father supported her in that. He used to say, 'Education is the great equalizer.' While my father may not have had a formal education, he was always wise."

Cantu's parents also nurtured in their children the idea that no one owed them anything. "It was," says Cantu, "our responsibility to do the best we could. They

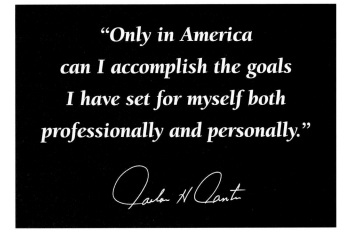

"Only in America can I accomplish the goals I have set for myself both professionally and personally."

taught us to work hard, demand responsibility, and take the initiative. I never felt I was at a disadvantage in the areas that mattered. I felt I could compete if I just worked hard enough."

While it was not required of him, young Cantu was always encouraged to work. His first job was selling pumpkins and squash when he was only 10. As soon as he got a bicycle, however, he got a paper

route. After delivering papers for four years, he worked for Western Union as a delivery boy. He also worked at the Ford dealership each summer as a laborer, sanding cars and doing janitorial work.

Cantu was an active student in high school. He served as vice president of his junior and senior class, and was co-captain of the football team. As a freshman he met his future wife, Glo-

ria. "I slacked off a bit in school after I met Gloria. We had a great time," says Cantu.

In 1951, Cantu entered Texas A&M, an all-male institution at the time, and majored in agricultural economics. To earn his way through school, Cantu worked for the athletic department as a janitor. Later, he worked for the U.S. Department of Agriculture, where he thought he could learn some-

thing that would help him get a job after he finished his education.

Upon graduation, Cantu married Gloria, then went to work for Cook & Co., a cotton trading firm. It was there that Cantu had his first mentor in his professional life. Ned Cook, a delegator to those he thought would respond positively to his challenges, taught young Cantu to never be afraid to take a risk.

The firm sent Cantu to Mexico, as well as Central and South America, where Cantu managed some of the firm's Latin American operations. Because Cantu was successful at his job, Cook then asked him to facilitate the acquisition of a Mexican pest-control company. Cantu and his wife settled in Mexico City and began raising their six children. By the early 1970s, however, the Cantus found Catholic schools in Mexico City to be prohibitively expensive. They decided it would be in the best interests of their children's education to return to the States. Cantu took a job in Indianapolis as branch manager of a Cook subsidiary, Terminix.

Cantu quickly moved up the ladder at Terminix, and became president and COO in 1978. At the time, Ter-

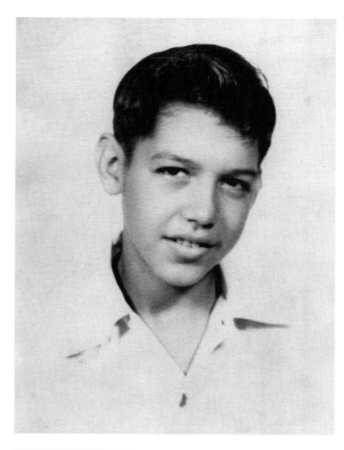

Carlos Cantu in the seventh grade at St. Joseph's Academy.

Cantu's graduation from Texas A&M University.

minix was a distant second in the pest-control industry. Cantu's goal was to become number one, but everyone told him it would be impossible to accomplish. Cantu set about establishing an organizational culture that focused on the dignity and worth of individuals, the pursuit of excellence, and economic performance as a tool to achieve goals. Cantu's leadership transformed the company and within five years, Terminix was the number one pest-control business nationwide.

When Cook decided to sell Terminix in 1986, Cantu helped the new buyer, ServiceMaster. Not knowing if he would still have a job after the sale went through, Cantu got top dollar for Terminix. Bill Pollard, the head of ServiceMaster, talked for two hours with Cantu. In addition to discussing the company, they talked about personal values and business philosophy. Pollard learned Cantu's commitment to truth, dignity, and quality closely matched his own. After holding a number of high-level jobs in ServiceMaster's consumer services division, Cantu became president and CEO of ServiceMaster in 1994.

Today, ServiceMaster provides consumer services to nearly six million customers through five major companies: Tru-Green/ChemLawn, Terminix, Merry Maids, ServiceMaster Residential and Commercial Services, and American Home Shield. ServiceMaster also is the leading provider of facilities support services to the health care, education, and business and industrial markets. This year, ServiceMaster was named by *Worth* magazine as one the country's top 50 "blue chip" stocks.

Carlos Cantu, one of only six Hispanics to head a Fortune 500 company, says his success is indicative of the opportunities that seem to be unique to this country. "I have lived and worked in other countries, and I don't know that there is any other place where this type of success can happen. I don't mean just financial success. I mean the environment for my overall feeling of accomplishment. To me, success equals respect. To have the respect of my associates and friends is the greatest feeling one can have."

In addition, Cantu enjoys the success of his family. He and Gloria, married for 40 years now, have six children. "Our children think of each other as friends, and they see Gloria and me as their friends, too. My wife has been a

Carlos and Gloria Cantu were married in 1956.

Cantu graded cotton during his early years in the cotton trading business.

21

Cantu checking a Mexican soybean field in 1965.

strong supporter of me. We feel the same way about each other now as we did in high school. Our family is wholesome, positive, and based on values. That's how I define success."

When Cantu heard about his Horatio Alger Award, he said, "Recognition in this country knows no bounds. You hear the statement 'only in America.' Well, it's true. As a first-generation American, I can tell you I am proud to be an American. I am proud of my heritage as well, but only in America can I accomplish the goals I have set for myself both professionally and personally. Only in America can I lay claim to my roots, my heritage, and my culture without being an isolationist."

In his community, Cantu serves on El Valor's Civic Leadership

Carlos Cantu is president and CEO of ServiceMaster, which serves six million customers through five major companies.

Team, which raises funds for citizens in Chicago's inner city. Cantu says of his involvement with the organization, "We are keeping people from being isolated. We help them to help themselves. I like to focus on the individual." He also serves on the board of DePaul University and is a trustee of the Assisi Foundation and the Field Museum of Chicago.

Cantu strongly agrees with his father when he says that in this country if you are willing to prepare yourself for it, opportunity is still available. "To do that," says Cantu, "you must focus on education. As you develop, do so with wisdom and respect to the dignity of your fellow man. We all have a responsibility to succeed and to help those less fortunate than us to reach their full potential." ◆

Carlos and Gloria Cantu at their home in Memphis, Tennessee in 1992.

Gloria and Carlos Cantu at the inauguration of the Cantu Family Library, which they donated to St. Joseph's Academy.

Greeting Pope John Paul II at the Vatican in 1993.

MARY HIGGINS CLARK

AUTHOR

"**O**nce upon a time" are words that have always enthralled Mary Higgins Clark, who remembers as a child sitting around the table at family gatherings listening to her Irish relatives tell story after story. "Some," she says, "were sad stories, and some were glad stories. Nothing was ever told simply. I sat there and drank them all in."

Born in the Bronx in 1929, Clark enjoyed a happy and secure early childhood. Her father owned and managed a popular Irish American pub, while her mother stayed home to raise their three children. They lived in what Clark describes as a "pleasant house in a nice neighborhood." Things quickly changed, however, when the Depression came. Customers could no longer pay their bills, and the pub began to decline. Luke Higgins, Mary's father, could no longer afford to hire help. He went to work early, came home for an early supper, and then went back to work until late at night. Finally, his 20-hour days caught up with him and he died of a heart attack when Mary was only 10. She says of that time, "I was a Daddy's girl. We had a very special relationship, and I've missed him all my life."

Clark's parents had married late in life, both in their 40s. When her father died, her mother, Nora Higgins, received $2,000 in insurance, which would not go far to pay the mortgage on the house as well as the family's expenses. In her mid-50s, Nora was unable to find work. She tried to keep her lovely home by renting rooms, and a parade of tenants began to pass through the Higgins home. After three years of struggle, however, the family was forced to move into a cramped, three-room apartment above a tailor's shop. Still, Nora Higgins did not feel sorry for herself. "Her motto," says Clark, "was no matter how bad things are, they will be better tomorrow." Watching her mother show so much courage taught young Clark resilience. Even today, Clark says the characters in her books are resilient and resourceful. "When calamity strikes," she says, "they carry on." Little did she know at the time that one day Mary would face a similar fate to her mother's, and would fall back on the example her mother had shown during a difficult time.

Education was the one value most prized by Nora Higgins. "My mother worked from the time she was 13 until she married, but she always took college courses at night," says Clark. Enrolled in a Catholic school, Clark showed a talent for writing from an early age. "My mother thought everything I wrote was priceless," says Clark. "I was in a poem-writing stage when I was seven. When relatives visited, my mother would say, 'Mary has written a beautiful new poem. Mary, stand up and recite that lovely poem.' That kind of encouragement was important to my development and it gave me a strong self-image." Mary continued writing and became known as a great storyteller. She recalls, "When I went to pajama parties, I would tell stories that began: 'Some one is standing behind that curtain, watching. His eyes will fall on one of us. I wonder which one . . .'"

Clark won a scholarship to an exceptional girls' academy. While there as a teenager, she worked as a switchboard operator and babysitter. She elected to defer college because she was anxious to find work and contribute to household finances. Her feeling of responsibility to her family increased when her older brother Joseph died while serving in World War II. He was only 18. "He was such a special person," says Clark. "He

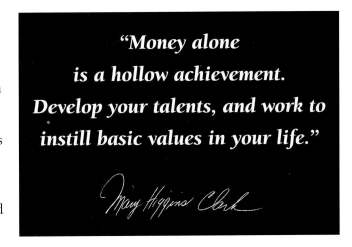

"*Money alone is a hollow achievement. Develop your talents, and work to instill basic values in your life.*"

Mary Higgins Clark

was president of his class, and the lead in the school play. It was very hard for my mother to lose him. Losing my father and brother taught me what is most important in this world, and that's counting heads at the end of the day. Life is fragile and can end without warning, so your family and those close to you are what is most important."

Clark enrolled in the Woods Secretarial School. When she finished her

course of study, she landed a job as an advertising assistant at Remington Rand. Three years later, she ran into an old friend who was an airline flight attendant. Clark became intrigued with travel when her friend said, "God, it was beastly hot in Calcutta." With those seven words Clark was hooked—she wanted to see the world and got a job with Pan Am. Her run was Europe, Africa, and Asia. "I was in a revolution in Syria and on the last flight into Czechoslovakia before the Iron Curtain went down," Clark recalls. After one year, she married an old friend, Warren Clark, a salesman in the travel industry.

Within the first eight years of their marriage, Clark gave birth to five children. Even so, she felt a compelling need to write. Soon after her marriage, she had signed up for a creative writing

class at New York University, where her professor advised her to write about something with which she was familiar. She began to use flight attendants as main characters in her short stories for magazines. After 40 rejections, she sold her first story for $100.

Ten years after they married, Warren was diagnosed with severe arteriosclerosis, and was told he would not survive the condition. Says Clark, "We spent the next five years knowing there was an ax over his head, but those were the best years of our 15-year marriage. We did exactly what we wanted to do and saw only people we liked. We gave all our free time to each other and to the children." In 1964, Warren suffered his third heart attack in five years and died. Clark became a widow when she was only 34, and her five children ranged in age from five to 13. Warren's mother was visiting at the time and, realizing he was dying, suffered a fatal heart attack.

Clark tried to teach her children to remember the joyful times with their father. "We had a very happy household. Warren was the funniest man I had ever known. I knew it would be an

Mary Higgins Clark with brother Joseph.

Clark poses with her brother on confirmation day.

insult to his memory to go around with a long face." Still, major financial worries were imminent. Warren's ill health had made him uninsurable, so Mary Clark needed to work to support their family and took a job writing radio scripts during the day. She also decided that she wanted to write books and began her routine of getting up at 5 a.m. to write, before getting the kids ready for school and commuting to her job.

One radio job Clark held for three years was scripting biographies for a daily program called *Portrait of a Patriot.* That job led to Clark's first venture into full-length book writing. She completed a biography of George Washington titled *Aspire to the Heavens* in 1969. Unfortunately, the lofty title led bookstore owners to shelve it with inspirational works, and the book was a commercial failure.

Realizing that the majority of books she enjoyed reading were thrillers and mysteries, Clark decided to try her own hand at those genres. "It was like a prospector stumbling on a vein of gold," she says. She became inspired by a true murder case in the news at the time and wrote *Where Are the Children?* Two publishing houses rejected the book before Simon & Schuster finally accepted and promoted it. The book became a bestseller when it appeared in 1975. Paperback rights gave Clark a check for $100,000, which she knew would see to her children's college education. She also used the money for her own education. At the age of 44, Clark enrolled in Fordham University. Four years later she graduated *summa cum laude* with a degree in philosophy. She threw herself a graduation party, and her invitations proclaimed her own philosophy of life: "This invitation is 25 years overdue—help prove it's not too late."

Clark's superstardom in the world of suspense was clinched when she made her first $1 million with her second novel, *A Stranger Is Watching*. Today, Mary Higgins Clark is this country's top bestselling woman suspense writer, and also enjoys great popularity internationally. In addition to those mentioned, her bestsellers include *The Cradle Will Fall*; *A Cry in the Night*; *Stillwatch*; *Weep No More, My Lady*; *Loves Music, Loves to Dance*; *All Around the Town*; *I'll Be Seeing You*; *Remember Me*; *The Lottery Winner*; *Let Me Call You Sweetheart*; *Silent*

Mary Higgins Clark (first row, center) with her brothers and cousins.

Mary Higgins Clark at 21.

Clark with husband Warren and their five children.

Mary Higgins Clark poses in front of a bookstore in England while on her first book tour.

Night; Moonlight Becomes You; and *My Gal Sunday.* Nine of her books have been made into movies, and Clark made a cameo appearance in the most recent adaptation, *While My Pretty One Sleeps.*

Recently, Clark married John Conheeney, a retired Wall Street executive. "My daughter, Patricia Clark Derenzo, introduced us and it was right from day one," she says. "We met on St. Patrick's Day and got married in November."

When asked about her success, Clark says she was never one to put off what she felt she needed to do. "So many would-be writers say, 'As soon as I raise my kids, I'll write; as soon as I retire, I'll write.' *As soon as* are the three fatal words in the English language," says Clark. She advises young people to take their education seriously and avoid cutting corners. She adds, "Money alone is a hollow achievement. Develop your talents, and work to instill basic values in your life. Follow your dream, and don't put off what you hanker to do."

Clark says her Horatio Alger Award is an honor she holds in high esteem. "My books have enjoyed great success," she says, "but other good writers often don't make it. I remind the Lord everyday I am thankful for my success and I am not getting arrogant."

Clark is reminded of "Suspense Writer of the Year" Isaac Bashevis Singer, who said unless you are a storyteller, you are not a writer. He went on to say that in medieval times, the storyteller went from castle to castle and always began with the magical words: "Once upon a time," and everyone would shush each other and pull closer to the fire. "I am a storyteller," says Clark. "Just put that on my tombstone and I'll be happy." ◆

After the sale of her first thriller, Clark enrolled in college and graduated Fordham University summa cum laude *at the age of 48.*

Clark holds her first grandchild.

Clark today with husband John Conheeney and their blended family.

ROBERT L. CRANDALL

CHAIRMAN AND CEO
AMR CORPORATION/AMERICAN AIRLINES, INC.

A long-time leader of the airline industry, Robert Crandall has two qualities that have helped make him a success. One of them is integrity—he says what he means and delivers what he promises. Another is his commitment to excellence. He credits his parents with instilling these virtues in him at the earliest age. "My parents' values," says Crandall, "were absolutist. There were no compromises. You told the truth, you did what you said you would do, you lived the straight and narrow, and you did everything as well as you could. I've done well living by those standards."

Crandall was born in 1935 in a small community in Rhode Island. "It was nothing more than a wide spot in the road," he says. "We didn't even have a store." He lived with his family on one end of a potato field, which was owned by his father's parents, who lived on the other end of the field. He remembers his father built their house, and even dug the basement out by hand.

Crandall describes his parents as "protectively Calvinist." "My father was a hard-edged sort of man. You did it right, or you paid the consequences. My mother had the same values, but she softened his edges now and then to my benefit." Crandall recalls a time when as a child he stole a pumpkin on Halloween night. His father marched him by the ear down to the fellow he stole it from and demanded that he apologize for the prank.

Crandall's father worked throughout the Depression years on government-sponsored construction projects. "My father was an engineer who worked on various projects for the Civilian Conservation Corps," says Crandall. When World War II started, Crandall's father worked for a company that supplied hand tools for the Seabees. After the war, he went into the insurance business, a career choice that resulted in numerous moves across the United States. Young Crandall attended 14 schools in 12 years, which regularly put him in the position of having to prove himself. "If nothing else, it taught me to adapt well to changing situations," says Crandall. Still, when he graduated from high school in 1953, Crandall's schoolmates voted him "best student," "most ambitious," and, surprisingly, "most affectionate boy."

The virtues of hard work and thrift were highly valued in the Crandall household. At the age of 14, Crandall remembers one of his first jobs was digging a foundation for a house in North Carolina. He also had a paper route throughout his childhood. In high school, Crandall worked in grocery stores. He continued to work in college, even though he had an academic scholarship to the College of William and Mary in Virginia. To pay for personal expenses, Crandall was a waiter for the Williamsburg Foundation's Kings Arms Tavern, for which he dressed daily in 18th century garb.

After three semesters at William and Mary, Crandall wanted to return to Rhode Island and his high school sweetheart, Jan Schmults. "I couldn't afford to hitchhike back and forth to see her any longer,"

says Crandall. He transferred to the University of Rhode Island and earned his degree in business administration, covering expenses by waxing and buffing the cafeteria floor each day and holding other part-time jobs.

After graduation, Crandall married Jan and immediately reported to Ft. Benning, Georgia. "Our honeymoon," says Crandall, "was the drive down to the base." Jan

worked as a nurse while Crandall finished his six-month tour of duty. Upon his release, he worked briefly for the John Hancock Mutual Life Insurance Company in Philadelphia, but quickly realized it wasn't what he wanted to do for the rest of his life. His dream was to attend law school, but he couldn't afford it. Instead, he accepted the offer of an Arthur Young scholarship to the University of Pennsylvania's

Wharton School of Business. He attended school during the day, and was "night manager" of a radio station.

Crandall's first job out of graduate school was with Eastman Kodak Company as a credit representative. When he was told it would take 20 years to become a vice president with the company, an ambitious Crandall left and went to do the same work for Hallmark in Kansas City.

"Leadership isn't about doing it all yourself, but about involving other people to use their full capabilities and achieve a shared vision."

Soon after he arrived, Crandall was asked if he would run the company's computer programming division. "I didn't know anything about computers, but it sounded like a good opportunity, and I was willing to learn." That decision became a turning point in Crandall's career.

After three years at Hallmark, Crandall took a job at TWA as assistant treasurer in charge of credit operations. Three

years later, he transferred to the airline's headquarters in New York, and soon afterwards was given the job of running the airline's data processing operations. The great crisis of the time was TWA's lack of a computerized reservations system. Crandall oversaw the installation of a system that made the company competitive with other airlines. After the data processing job, Crandall became TWA's controller and then left the airline industry to serve as a senior vice president and treasurer for Bloomingdale's.

Crandall quickly realized the retail business was not for him, and after less than a year with Bloomingdale's, he left to become American Airline's chief financial officer. One of the most important contributions Crandall made early in his career with American was to upgrade the airline's data processing function. When Crandall arrived in 1974, the company's systems did not meet the same standards as many other airlines. He quickly fixed the deficiency, and led a push to put American's systems in the forefront of the industry's capabilities.

A year later, Crandall was named American's senior vice president for marketing. Crandall and

Bob Crandall in Evanston in 1944.

Bob Crandall, age 1, with his mother.

Crandall poses with his mother on his high school graduation day.

Robert L. Crandall

his staff tackled the problem of generating revenue from seats that were going unsold on many flights. Their solution was super-saver airfares—deep discounts for tickets bought well in advance. The new approach kept American from being undercut by the charter airlines, and has since become a staple of airline marketing.

In 1980, when the airline industry was in the throes of a violent restructuring brought about by deregulation, Crandall became president of American. Crandall is noted for restructuring American's fleet, which gave the company more flexibility in its route system. He also created the industry's first frequent flyer program, called AAdvantage. The program gave American a jump on its competitors because it used American's data processing capabilities to make participation easy for American's customers. Other airlines matched the program, but took years to close American's lead.

During the 1980s, Crandall expanded the company dramatically and started setting up an international route system. Today, more than a third of American's revenue and more than 40 percent of its profits

come from international operations. Having taken over one of the least well-positioned airlines in the early days of deregulation, Bob Crandall—the only airline executive still in place from those days—has created a much larger, stronger, more competitive, and innovative company whose market share has nearly doubled in the last 20 years.

Crandall describes his management style as "collegial." He continues, "I like to talk with people to solve problems, so I have a lot of meetings. Still, I am a decisive person and my tendency is to sort a problem out and then act to fix it." Crandall is not an isolated leader. His leadership style within American is group-oriented. He says, "One of the most important qualities of leadership is to recognize that you use leadership to empower others. It isn't about doing it all yourself, but about involving other people to achieve a shared vision." He is proud of the fact that several former American managers have gone on to become high-ranking executives at other airlines.

While his attention to detail is legendary, Crandall has remained on top longer than anyone else largely because of his ability to see the big picture and anticipate

Crandall's schoolmates voted him "Most Ambitious" and "Best Student."

Robert Crandall married Margaret Jan Schmults in 1957.

Crandall says he uses leadership to include others to achieve a shared vision.

Crandall enjoys a company picnic.

changes about to take place. His willingness to change whatever needs to be changed to achieve his goal has also been critically important. "You can't be afraid to rock the boat," he says.

According to Crandall, "you have to have the highest ethical standards to be an effective leader." He credits his parents with instilling in him the standards by which he lives each day of his life. He also says his wife Jan had a strong and positive influence. "We've been married since prehistoric times," he jokes, "but we have a parallel set of values. We've raised three great kids, and have four wonderful grandchildren. We treat people the way we want to be treated, which is a simple philosophy but one that works."

Crandall presides at ceremony for new international service.

Robert L. Crandall

Crandall's advice for today's young people is to take full advantage of their years in school. "Get the best education you can," he says. "Read the great books, especially history and biographies, and learn to write and speak effectively. With a solid foundation, you will have the basics for learning anything else you want or need. Everyone in the world is looking for capable people. So get the basics of a good education, choose something you like to do, and work hard at being the best in your chosen field."

Crandall says his Horatio Alger award is gratifying. "It's nice to have one's achievements recognized, and being invited to join a group of such distinguished people is a great honor." ◆

Crandall with acclaimed pianist Van Cliburn and Cliburn's mother.

Crandall volunteering to improve a neighborhood in Fort Worth.

Robert Crandall with his wife Jan.

MICHAEL S. EGAN

CHAIRMAN AND CEO
ALAMO RENT A CAR

Born in Milwaukee, Wisconsin in 1940, Michael Egan had to grow up more quickly than most children. Before he even had a driver's license, Egan, out of necessity, started to assume responsibility for managing a family business while also trying to help care for his family members. He didn't realize that the sales and management experience he was accruing at the age of 16 would serve him well when, years later, he would build one of the largest car rental businesses in the world.

Egan easily remembers the atmosphere that permeated Milwaukee during the 1940s. "First, the war years and the pulling together. Sons at war, victory gardens, war bonds, worry. Then things started getting better. Folks had some money, new cars, trips, confidence. It was just like *Happy Days* with the Fonz," says Egan. Settled largely by Germans, the city, Egan remembers, had beautiful parks and gardens. "While my family is not German, I admired these people and embraced their culture of planning and hard work."

Egan spent much of his childhood divided between Milwaukee and Florida. Every other year, his mother took the three boys to live with her father in Florida. The moves required big adjustments to different schools and many attempts to reestablish old friendships. It was exciting for young Egan, but difficult. Still, Florida is where Egan had his first mentor in life, his Grandfather Shenners. "He helped me understand how to think abstractly, how to move from what you know and don't know to what might be. He helped me establish my creativity," says Egan.

Florida is where Egan began his first job at the age of nine. "I sold coconuts on U.S. 1, which was the main route into Florida before interstates. All the snow birds passed by my stand on their way to escape East Coast winters," recalls Egan. On their way home, however, no one wanted coconuts, so Egan switched to selling the Sunday *Miami Herald* in the late spring. Egan fondly remembers

Easter Sunday as his most profitable sales day. "I got my papers at 11:00 p.m., the day before Easter. I would stay up all night assembling the papers. Then at 3:30 a.m., my parents would load two cars and drive me over to the sunrise service held each year on the beach. When people started arriving, I sold my papers. I would gross more in that one day than I did during the whole winter of regular selling at churches on Sunday morning. This was my first lesson in 'Make hay while the sun shines!'"

Family life for Egan was confusing and often strained. There was real love but also real stress. "We had a pretty serious alcohol problem at home," says Egan. His father, Tom, a lawyer in the surety bond business, was the man who would mentor him in business during his teenage years. Egan's mother, Marcia, was an artist and businesswoman. She wore her love on her sleeve and had utter confidence in her son. "One of my fond childhood memories was listening to my parents discuss business at the dining room table," Egan says. The family's business orientation influenced Egan early in his life and he began his own business as a morning newsboy. Rising at

4:00 a.m., he delivered papers, went to school, and played sports. "But as the eldest child," says Egan, "I was responsible for more than just growing up. I helped manage the family. You do these things because you see the need, and you are the only one there to do it. That's my growing-up story. It was hard going much of the time. It was also fun and challenging. I guess most kids find that true. You live the life

When Egan was 14, his family decided to build and operate a family amusement park in Wisconsin Dells. An avid gardener, Tom created a beautifully landscaped park, while Marcia helped create the fantasy. She oversaw the creation of the attractions for what became Storybook Gardens. "This was a hybrid park," says Egan. "At first there was noth-

ing else like it. Families would come to the Dells from Chicago on their summer vacation. Storybook Gardens was strategically located so the vacationers had to pass our park to get to the lake country and the North Woods."

By the time he was 16, Egan, who managed the park's construction crew, was the operating manager of Storybook Gardens. The responsibility of "marketing

director" also fell squarely on his shoulders. He drove all day delivering brochures to gas stations, roadside restaurants, and motels. The competition for tourism dollars was fierce, and he learned how to sell and market in the heat of the battle.

Working at the amusement park gave Egan a nest egg toward his college education. He wanted to attend a school where he could major in

tourist management, but the closest thing he could find was hotel administration at Cornell University. To earn his expenses, Egan was a bartender and also managed a small restaurant. Academically, however, things didn't go so well. "I felt like a duck out of water," says Egan. The too-technical training he was receiving in his major contrasted dramatically with the classical high school education he had had in the hands of the Jesuits at Marquette High School. "And," he admits, "I partied a bit too much. Bad combination." He flunked out of school during his sophomore year. This was an eye-opening experience and once again Egan took control of his destiny. After writing the dean of Cornell a letter saying that he promised to keep at least a 90 percent average if he could continue there, Egan was reinstated. He did well from that point on. Tapping into his creativity that was inspired by his mother and nurtured by his grandfather, Egan became an adept designer. He began designing food facilities, and won a national award for his efforts.

After college, Egan entered the Army Reserves. He served as chief wardmaster of a

"Put God and family first. I have dedicated my life's work to the greater glory of God."

Michael S. Egan

you got and make the best of it."

Michael Egan, age 2.

Michael Egan with his father Tom and his mother Marcia.

Michael Egan's home in Lake Worth, Florida. They moved every other year until he was in high school.

1,000-bed general hospital. After receiving his discharge from the Army in 1969, Egan left the family business to pursue a design career. He designed food facilities for Yale University and helped manage the school's food service and other administration functions. "At Yale," recalls Egan, "I learned life's lesson of social class segregation. There were Brahmins and untouchables. You were a Brahmin if you had a Ph.D., and an untouchable if you didn't. I was an untouchable, but I didn't want, nor could I afford, five more years of classes. I left Yale to try teaching without a Ph.D. at the University of Massachusetts." He got a job as an instructor at their

hotel school. He also ran the student union and the continuing education food service.

After 10 years of academia, Egan realized he was not content. "I was 32 years old, had essentially two jobs, was married with three children, and could not cover all the bills," says Egan. It was then that an old friend from Cornell asked if he would be interested in running the Florida division of Olin's, a car rental business based in New York, which the friend's family had recently acquired. "Yes" was Egan's answer.

Egan moved his family to Florida, and for the next three years built Olin's Florida business to a big success. When the parent

Storbyook Gardens, Wisconsin Dells, Wisconsin.

Michael Egan is ready to greet guests at Storybook Gardens.

Michael Egan as a high school senior.

company, headquartered in New York, went bankrupt, Egan was made president of the overall operation by the creditor committee. He left his family in Florida and headed for New York to put his management skills to work. He turned around the company and attained profitability, but had to sell the whole operation to pay trust taxes. Egan says of that time, "I wanted to buy Olin's Florida business, but they wouldn't sell to me. I was supporting my family paycheck to paycheck. That's when I realized I had to find a way to own my own business."

Within two weeks, Egan approached 76-year-old billionaire John MacArthur who had a failing 400-car rental operation in Florida called Alamo. He went to work for MacArthur and negotiated an option to buy Alamo at a later date if he could make the business profitable. Egan accomplished that goal within four months, but MacArthur died before Egan was able to buy the company. The executors of MacArthur's estate tried to sell the company out from under Egan, but Egan was determined to reach his goal of owning a business.

After quickly pulling together a group of investors to buy Alamo from MacArthur's estate, Egan became a minority shareholder and president of the company in 1978. To grow the company, Egan pursued an undeveloped niche, the

Michael Egan served in the Army in the late 1960s.

leisure traveler. He courted travel agents and paid them commissions to use Alamo. To be vacationer-friendly, Alamo was one of the first companies to offer unlimited free mileage. The business went from obscurity to being one of the largest car rental companies in the world. Its fleet of cars grew from 400 to more than 165,000, with 123 North American locations and 100 international offices.

In a surprise move last fall, Egan, who had become the majority shareholder, sold Alamo to Republic Industries. He continues to serve as chairman and CEO of Alamo. Egan also owns a majority investment in Nantucket Nectars, a bottled fruit juice company; Certified Vacations; and a small Nantucket inn.

When asked about his success, Egan says, "I don't think success is a point or a mark on the wall. I don't think, for example, that when you've made a million dollars you are a success. It is what you do every day that adds value to your life and the lives of those around you that is important. If you are using your God-given talents in a way that pushes you to do better and better, then you are succeeding. There are no arbitrary markers you can hit that say 'success.' Instead, success is the ability to get up when you are knocked down, and developing and using your talents to a point of real accomplishment."

Egan's advice for young people is to "have a plan and work very hard every day. At all times, you must be true to yourself. For-

Egan is an accomplished artist.

Michael Egan with his wife Jacqueline.

Michael Egan

mulate a dream objective and focus your daily attention toward it. Be creative. Learn how to control the power you have over yourself. While we each have the power to be destructive to ourselves, we also have the power to lift up ourselves. It's a power we must understand and control. Value and preserve your reputation and your health. Put God and family first. Since my Jesuit days I have dedicated my life's work to the greater glory of God."

Egan gets great satisfaction from his family. He has three daughters and two sons. He speaks of his wife Jacqueline with pride and love. "Jacqueline is my friend and most avid supporter. She helps me focus on the great good that life can offer."

Of his Horatio Alger Award, Egan says, "I am honored to be in such accomplished company. When I was growing up I always had mentors. I still do. These wise people help me to understand myself and the world. The Horatio Alger Scholars are in need of mentoring at this point in their lives as they make their first critical choices—how they will educate themselves, the work they will do, who they will marry, where they will live. At the same time, they are themselves mentors for their peer group because they are already beginning to shine. They are shining examples of working hard to make their dreams come true. A large part of whatever I am today is due to the mentoring I received throughout my life. I am looking forward to serving as a mentor to the Horatio Alger Scholars." ◆

The Egans with their two sons.

Michael Egan enjoying the Nantucket farm he designed and built.

Michael Egan's wife Jacqueline poses with their five children, two grandchildren, one son-in-law, and two dogs.

ALAN "ACE" GREENBERG

CHAIRMAN
BEAR STEARNS

Dubbed one of the shrewdest players on Wall Street, Alan Greenberg was born in Wichita, Kansas in 1927. He moved with his family to Oklahoma City when he was six years old. At a time when the country was mired in the economic destruction of the Depression, Greenberg's father was determined to be successful. The move to Oklahoma City was a chance for him to start a new women's apparel store, which later grew into a chain.

Greenberg describes his family as close-knit. His parents, he says, instilled in their children the values of hard work, responsibility, and charity. "I had a sensational mother and father," says Greenberg. In fact, his solid upbringing may be what gives him the emotional strength to survive and prosper today in the frantic investment banking business. "I've never forgotten my roots," he says. "All four of my grandparents came to America from Russia, trying to escape hunger. They didn't know what to expect when they got here. It took a great deal of courage for them to make that journey, and I admire them for it."

An excellent student and athlete, Greenberg was a halfback on his high school football team and helped them win the Oklahoma state championship. He also did well in track, winning city and district championships for two years in a row in the 100- and 220-yard dashes. "I enjoyed school," Greenberg says. "I got good grades and loved math."

When he was in junior high and high school, Greenberg worked in his father's store, mostly in the credit department. One summer he remembers driving a truck so that he could "beef up" for football.

It was football that took Greenberg to the University of Oklahoma on a scholarship. During his freshman year, however, an injury to his back cut short Greenberg's football career. He transferred to the University of Missouri and majored in "getting out." It was during college that Greenberg developed a passion for playing bridge. He earned a degree in business administration in 1949 and headed for New York City.

After reading *The Robber Barons*, Greenberg had become fascinated with Wall Street and hoped to break into the financial world. New York was the only place to go. His uncle asked a Wichita oil man living in New York to write five letters of recommendation for Greenberg. "Basically," says Greenberg, "the letters said 'I don't know this young man, but I know his uncle and if his uncle says he is an outstanding young man, I'd appreciate any courtesy you could give him.'"

With his letters in hand, Greenberg traveled to New York, where he didn't know a single person, and dropped off his letters at five investment firms. Only one, Bear Stearns, offered him a job. "I wasn't from an Ivy League school, so my services weren't exactly in demand," he says.

Starting as a clerk in the oil department making $32.50 a week wasn't exactly the exciting adventure Greenberg had in mind, but he didn't stay in that position for long. Six months later, Greenberg maneuvered himself into a clerk position in the arbitrage

department. Soon, Greenberg showed remarkable trading skills. By the time he was 25, he was running the department. In addition, Greenberg began managing the firm's money. This gave him great exposure to the firm's partners, who liked what they saw.

When Greenberg was 31, two major events happened—one would put him on top of the financial world; the other had the ability to bring it

all crashing down. Greenberg was named a partner of Bear Stearns, and he was diagnosed with a cancer that had less than a 50 percent survival rate. Greenberg faced both challenges with his usual courage and confidence. He underwent surgery and began months of convalescence. For the next 12 years he had checkups at the Mayo Clinic every six months. Greenberg beat the odds against him, but he

doesn't spend time dwelling on the past. His eye is on the present and bringing in new business to Bear Stearns. In 1978, Greenberg was named chief executive officer of the firm. He continued to expand the business, finally taking it public in 1985. Greenberg was named chairman and CEO. Today, Greenberg retains the title of chairman of the board and chairman of the executive committee.

Under Greenberg's direction, Bear Stearns has become the fifth largest investment banking firm in the United States on the basis of equity capital. Employment has grown from 1,200 employees to 7,800. The firm has never had a losing year and consistently has one of the highest returns on equity of any Wall Street firm. In addition to the many honors his success has brought him, Green-

berg was knighted by the queen of Denmark.

When asked about his tremendous success, Greenberg is honest about what made it happen. "I have good genes. I'm smart. Still, I liked my work. I had a tremendous desire to be successful so I worked very hard."

Greenberg thinks opportunities are greater now than when he started. "You have to pick something you love to do or you won't win. You will be competing against people who may be intellectually inferior to you but if they like what they are doing, they're going to beat you every time. You have to work hard."

While he works hard at the office, Greenberg has a good time outside of it. Bridge, a game he learned in college, is still a consuming passion. Often, Greenberg leaves work at the end of the day and spends a few hours playing bridge at the Regency Whist Club. It's a game he takes seriously. His wife Kathy says she does not hesitate to call her husband at the office, but she would not think of disturbing him during a bridge game. Greenberg compares bridge to his line of work, saying, "All business is calculated risk, and bridge is taking calculated risks."

> *"Try to give more than you take."*
>
> *Alan Greenberg*

43

Alan "Ace" Greenberg

Alan Greenberg with his mother and brother.

Greenberg in Wichita, Kansas.

Greenberg showed athletic talent early in life.

Greenberg as a young boy.

An accomplished amateur magician, Greenberg is easily enticed to perform a few illusions. He says of his hobby, "I've been involved in magic all my life." He even seems to have a magical touch with his dogs. "Kathy and I get up in the morning and if the weather's nice out, I train my dogs." When asked what he does when the weather is not nice, Greenberg replies, "I train my dogs."

In addition to business and hobbies, Greenberg says family has always been an important part of his life. Following a divorce from his first wife, Greenberg was a bachelor for 12 years before marrying Kathryn Olson, an attorney. A proud father, Greenberg has a son and daughter from his first marriage. "My daughter holds the distinction of being the first female member of the American Stock Exchange. My son runs the arbitrage department of a bank in New York."

Greenberg is flattered by his Horatio Alger Award. Looking back over his life, he says, "I have always tried to be very fair. I make it a point that anyone who has known me has a good taste in their mouth. To do that, I give more than I take." ◆

Greenberg attended college on a football scholarship.

Greenberg (center) poses with his family.

45

Greenberg won district championships in the 100- and 200-yard dashes.

Greenberg in Colorado enjoying a favorite fishing hole.

Greenberg and his dogs visiting with disadvantaged kids.

Alan "Ace" Greenberg

Greenberg with his mother.

Alan Greenberg with his wife Kathy.

Greenberg shows his granddaughter Allison a magic trick.

Greenberg family poses with Israeli Prime Minister Netanyahu.

John "Jack" Grundhofer

Chairman, President & CEO
First Bank System, Inc.

When Jack Grundhofer sat in his southern California grammar school dreaming of his future, he never would have imagined himself as a sort of superhero who would one day rescue a failing bank and build it into one of the strongest bank holding companies in the country. As if that weren't enough, there would be other unseen challenges ahead for young Grundhofer. But the strong value system instilled in him as a child would serve him well in overcoming the near-fatal tragedies that would later come his way.

Grundhofer's mother won $100 for giving birth to Jack, the second child born in 1939 in Los Angeles. His parents had recently moved to Glendale, California, leaving their farm life in Minnesota behind them.

Grundhofer's father became a bartender, and his mother worked as a housekeeper for a wealthy woman the Grundhofer family called Aunt Rose. "She was kind to us," says Grundhofer, who remembers receiving much-needed clothes from her for Christmas.

Grundhofer describes his mother as very religious—an active, practicing Catholic. "The church and the Catholic school," says Grundhofer, "were a big part of my growing-up years." Maybe because she and her husband had to work so hard to make ends meet, Grundhofer's mother felt strongly about her children's education. She and her husband sacrificed a great deal so that their three children could attend Catholic schools, where they felt they would receive the best education. In addition to his job as a bartender, Grundhofer's father worked nights at Douglas Aircraft during the war years. "As long as I can remember, my father always had at least two jobs and sometimes three. We didn't see a lot of him, but he was supportive of all my mother did and believed," says Grundhofer.

An excellent student, Grundhofer started school early, which meant he was small compared to his classmates. "I was always the last one picked for a team," he laughs. Academically, however, Grundhofer had few equals. He says the nuns at school were a guiding factor, as was the nurturing encouragement he constantly received from his mother. When Grundhofer was 12, the nuns felt he should test for the highly acclaimed Jesuit school in Los Angeles, Loyola High School. The tuition was high, but the Grundhofers saw it as an open door to opportunity for their eldest child.

Grundhofer was accepted to Loyola, to which he took an hour-long streetcar ride each day. After school, he hurried back to Glendale and his job as a stock boy in a department store. He worked there afternoons and evenings for three hours to help pay his school tuition. That first year at Loyola, Grundhofer was the number one student in the school.

When Grundhofer was in the seventh grade, his father suffered a massive heart attack. He was not expected to live, and Grundhofer's mother looked to young Jack to take on more responsibility for the family's livelihood. He asked for a raise at the department store where he worked

and, thanks to his dry sense of humor, Grundhofer says, "They understood my situation and gave me a raise from 75 cents an hour to 85 cents." Happily, his father survived, but he was incapacitated for eight months. During the summer, Grundhofer worked full time so that his family would not lose their house. At night, he played baseball, a sport he was passionate about but had little time to play.

When he was 14, Grundhofer started to develop himself socially at school. "I was always such a bookworm," he says, "that I was lacking in social skills. I slipped to 15th in my class of 100, but I became a more well-rounded person." Grundhofer also discovered another side of life at Loyola. Most students came from well-to-do families, and he learned what education could do to propel him into a better life.

Upon graduation, Grundhofer was accepted to a number of schools, even the University of Southern California. But it was unrealistic for him to consider those offers. "I would have been taking money away from my brother and sister for their education," says Grundhofer. Instead, he accepted a baseball scholarship at Loyola University. He commuted to school in a car he bought when he was 17,

and collected pop bottles to pay for gas. After his sister began working, she often sent her brother money for gas and other necessities. To pay for expenses at school not covered by his scholarship, Grundhofer mowed lawns at the university.

With his degree in economics, Grundhofer looked for a job to pay off the $1,000 student loan his father had co-signed for him. He got a job at Union Bank mak-

ing $400 a month. He entered a general training program and began his real work for the bank—repossessing cars. "That wasn't a fun job, but you learn a lot about life," he says. To get himself into the prestigious credit training program at Union, Grundhofer needed more schooling. Within two years, he received his MBA in finance from the University of Southern California, which he attended at night.

He entered the two-year credit program and found that he excelled at the work of judging and analyzing loans. It wasn't long before Union's president Carl Reichardt realized Grundhofer's potential and sent him to manage the newly opened Newport Beach office. "He took a chance on me," says Grundhofer. "I'd never managed anything in my whole life." From a tiny trailer office, Grundhofer built the branch to $100 million in deposits in two years. "Carl Reichardt was, after my mother, my second mentor. He believed in me and encouraged me. He also pointed out my shortcomings, which is sometimes the best advice a mentor can give. No matter what our talents, we can always benefit from an outside perspective."

"There are no entitlements in life. You should be rewarded for what you do— for your performance."

John F. Grundhofer

Jack Grundhofer with his parents, John and Laura, visiting his grandfather's home in Mora, Minnesota (July 1939).

John F. (Jack) Grundhofer at age 5.

Grundhofer married and had two daughters. He also found he enjoyed teaching banking. He taught night classes at Chapman College and Orange Coast College. During the summer, he taught a class for two weeks at the Pacific Coast Banking School sponsored by the University of Washington. In 1972, Reichardt left Union Bank and went to work for Wells Fargo Bank. Grundhofer took over his responsibilities as regional manager.

Six years later, Reichardt became president of Wells Fargo Bank and asked Grundhofer to come work for him. Grundhofer started as an executive vice president, in charge of the southern half of the state. In 1986, Grundhofer was made vice chairman and added to his responsibilities the wholesale banking business, which was worldwide.

Grundhofer was content and prepared to finish his career with Wells Fargo, but in 1990 he was asked to run First Bank System in Minneapolis. Once again, he found the challenge too enticing to ignore. "Get-

Grundhofer siblings (from left to right): Jerry at age 3, Joan at age 5, and Jack at age 8.

ting a chance to run a Fortune 500 company is a big opportunity," says Grundhofer. The bank, however, was in crisis and in drastic need of restructuring to ensure its survival.

In his first year at First Bank, Grundhofer sold $3 billion in assets, reduced expenses by $100 million, streamlined the workforce, replaced most of the bank's top managers, and raised $170 million in equity capital. Grundhofer says, "Carl Reichardt taught me that it doesn't take a lot of people to turn things around. It takes a few good people." By 1991 the company was clearly making a comeback. Since then, First Bank has acquired an agricultural credit company, numerous bond indenture businesses, and 15 banks, adding more than $22 billion in assets from Illinois to Colorado. "Once you get to the top in terms of performance, the challenge is to stay there. We want people to go from thinking we are a *good* company to thinking we are a *great* company."

Grundhofer once again has come out on top, but

At an early age, Jack was taught the value of hard work while spending time with his grandfather on the farm near Pierz, Minnesota.

Playing second base earned Jack Grundhofer a baseball scholarship at Loyola Marymount University.

Jack Grundhofer, Class of 1956, Loyola High School, Los Angeles, California.

not without a great deal of personal fortitude. During his first year at First Bank, one of Grundhofer's daughters was involved in a shooting incident in a hotel bar near the UC Berkeley campus, where she was attending school. A man entered the bar of the hotel and began shooting for no known reason. Grundhofer's daughter was shot six times, but was able to escape with the help of a friend. Amazingly, she survived her injuries. Later that year, Grundhofer was abducted while on his way to work. He was entering the parking garage when he was kidnapped at gunpoint. Made to drive to Wisconsin with a bomb strapped to his wrist, Grundhofer was left tied up in a sleeping bag. His kidnapper asked for $3 million in ransom. Grundhofer was able to free himself and call for help. The authorities have been unable to convict the suspect Grundhofer picked out of a line-up. "Those two incidents were the toughest times of my life," says Grundhofer. "I had to work

The Loyola High School Class of 1956 graduate, Jack Grundhofer, with his brother Jerry.

John Grundhofer

through those personal tragedies. Still, I tell people I'm the luckiest person alive. I've got my wife, my daughters, a grandson, my health, and a business that is highly respected. To understand it all, though, I got professional help and my wife Beverly helped me a great deal."

Grundhofer believes there are no entitlements in life. "You should be rewarded for what you do, for your performance," he says. "My advice is to create your own luck by working hard and working smart. You should choose something you like to do because you will be at it for a long time. I feel passionate about my work and want those around me to feel the same."

Grundhofer says of his Horatio Alger Award, "It's unbelievable. This organization is a change agent for its scholars. These kids have a chance to be real leaders and role models. What we can do in mentoring them can have a snowball effect. It's very exciting to think about—like a dream come true." ◆

Jack Grundhofer helping daughters Karen and Kathy hunt for Easter eggs in 1972.

Bev and Jack Grundhofer.

Jack with his parents, John and Laura Grundhofer.

Jon M. Huntsman

Chairman and CEO
Huntsman Corporation

Jon Huntsman's birth in 1937 was a tense scene played out in the rural setting of Blackfoot, Idaho. Blaine and Kathleen Huntsman were living with their one-year-old son Blaine, Jr. in a two-room basement house with no indoor plumbing when Kathleen went into labor two months early with her second child. A midwife delivered the four-pound baby, who appeared to be stillborn. When the doctor arrived 15 minutes later, he pronounced the baby dead and worked to save the mother. Blaine Huntsman took the advice of the midwife and alternately immersed his baby son in hot and cold water in an attempt to get his circulation going. Finally, the baby cried. "You could say I've been in and out of hot water from that day forward," says Jon Huntsman, the head of the world's largest privately held chemical company.

Throughout most of his childhood, Huntsman was raised in rural Idaho, where his father was a music teacher in public schools. Each fall, Huntsman remembers that the schools closed for two weeks so that the farmers and their children could harvest the potato crop before it would freeze in the ground. While they were not farmers, the Huntsmans did their share of picking potatoes. "You learned how to work for everything you received," says Huntsman. "We fished and hunted, not for fun, but because we had to get the winter food supply built up. It was a Spartan upbringing, but one that I respected immensely."

When Huntsman was 13, his father decided to return to college and get his doctorate degree at Stanford. He attended school on the GI Bill and received $120 a month for expenses. The Huntsman family lived on that meager allowance for the next three years. "Our house was a World War II Quonset hut with eight other families sharing the building, separated only by cardboard walls. We had 700 square feet," recalls Huntsman. Expected to help with the family's expenses,

Huntsman was responsible for the gas and upkeep of the family car, as well as family medical bills. During the eighth and ninth grades, he worked two jobs to meet his family obligations. After school, he worked at a restaurant washing dishes and waiting tables. When he finished there, he cleaned a meat market. At the end of ninth grade, he got a job with J. C. Penney, which he kept for five years.

Of that time, Huntsman says that he found strength in his relationship with his brother Blaine. He explains, "I regarded my brother as an ally and a partner. We had to make it through this tough time together. I think it developed in us a powerful work ethic and a sense of helping others. What little we had, we shared with others at the University. We always knew we had to help others as well as let them help us to make it through. I don't think much has changed over the years."

Huntsman has always been a devout Mormon, following the religion of his ancestors. His church, he says, was an anchor for him even though his parents were not active members.

Palo Alto, the city that services Stanford University, is an affluent

community, but Huntsman neither lived in nor even understood those superior living standards. Still, he competed on an equal footing with his peers in school and even served as student body president during his senior year at Palo Alto High School. His excellent grades won Huntsman two scholarships to the University of Pennsylvania's Wharton School of Finance, which only accepted 300 under-

graduates each year. It took young Huntsman a long way away from his high school sweetheart Karen, but he was grateful for the excellent educational opportunity. To pay for his expenses while in college, he delivered flowers for a florist and waited tables at a sorority.

As soon as he finished his studies, Huntsman married Karen and then entered the Navy. "I spent 17 of the first 24 months of my marriage out to

sea," he says. Huntsman left the service in 1961 as a lieutenant and entered the egg business with Karen's uncles in California. Looking for a replacement for cardboard containers, Huntsman pursued the idea of a plastic egg carton. By 1967, Huntsman was made president of the joint venture, which had Dow Chemical as a 50-percent partner. During that time, Huntsman went to the University of Southern

California at night to earn his master's in business administration.

By 1970 his family was growing, and Huntsman decided he wanted to form his own company, which would actually compete with the industrial giant Dow Chemical Company. It took him and his brother Blaine, his partner at the time, two years to build their first plant. Both had to mortgage their houses to get their start-up money.

Once their company was up and running, Huntsman headed for Washington, D.C., to accept a position with the Nixon administration as associate administrator with the Department of Health, Education, and Welfare (HEW). He worked there for seven months under Eliot Richardson. One of Huntsman's first projects was a program he initiated called Management by Objectives, which detailed ways to streamline the agency. It wasn't long before H. R. (Bob) Haldeman called Huntsman and asked him to come to work for the White House as the President's staff secretary. "I began a year of 12- to 15-hour days, including weekends, and was the President's assistant dealing with all White House budgets, certain White House personnel, briefing the President on all his meetings, and handling all White House administrative matters. Today, that same job is done by four or five people."

A year later, Huntsman was exhausted and concerned about his company back home, which was on the brink of bankruptcy. He left Washington in April 1972, two months before the Watergate break-in, and was re-appointed CEO of Huntsman Con-

"We will place into society assistance for those who suffer, hope for those who may need inspiration, and education for those who may feel the challenge but do not have the means."

Huntsman (left) with father and brother.

Jon Huntsman's mother, Kathleen.

his products. In 1982, in the middle of a major recession, Huntsman bought from the Shell Oil Company an ailing polystyrene plant, which he quickly turned into a profitable venture. In 1994, he closed his largest deal ever—the acquisition of Texaco's chemical business for $1 billion. Now divided into four companies, Huntsman Corporation is the largest privately owned chemical concern in the world and a global manufacturer of petrochemicals, rubber, surfactants (soaps, detergents), and packaging products.

The $5 billion company is still family-owned and operated. The Huntsmans have six sons and three daughters. Eight of the sons or sons-in-law are full-time executives with the business, while the daughters and daughters-in-law are busy raising the Huntsmans' 32 grandchildren (soon to be 34). Jon and Karen have always given their children a voice in the business, and the children remember voting on company issues while still in grade school.

No one is amazed by Huntsman's incredible financial success more than Huntsman himself. Still, he says, "Wealth was never the driving force. It's what my wealth

Jon Huntsman with his father and brother in Idaho.

tainer Corporation. "I spent the next couple of years trying to resuscitate our business," says Huntsman. He was successful beyond his dreams. The company developed a plastic container, known as the clamshell, which McDonald's bought to package their Big Mac hamburger. Huntsman Container went on to develop about 70 other major packaging products, including the first plates, bowls, dishes, and carry-out containers made from plastic.

Huntsman felt the next step was to buy businesses that manufactured the basic raw materials that went into can do for humanity that interests me." Huntsman is a firm believer in giving back to the community and has become one of the world's most generous philanthropists. After the 1988 earthquake in Armenia, he built a concrete plant there to provide housing for 100,000 people left homeless. "He's given back more than anyone I've ever known," says Senator Orrin Hatch of Utah, who recalls once seeing Huntsman literally give a homeless man the coat off his back.

Recently, Huntsman gave the largest single gift to medical research—$100,000 million for cancer research. "We're building the Huntsman Cancer Institute in Utah to study and develop cures for familial cancer. We want to understand how the transfer of genes from one generation to the next causes certain families to be at high risk for cancer," says Huntsman. His focus on familial cancers comes from personal experience. Huntsman's mother died in his arms from breast cancer when she was in her 50s. His father died of prostate cancer. Huntsman himself has had two bouts with the dreaded disease. Like his father, he had prostate cancer in 1992, then developed lip

Jon Huntsman as student body president at Palo Alto High School.

Huntsman takes part in the Spoon Award at the University of Pennsylvania.

cancer a year later. Both are in remission.

Utah, it turns out, is a perfect place for this type of research to take place. Mormons, the predominant religious group in the area, are noted for their large families and meticulous family record keeping. "Our researchers will combine clinical care with research." Huntsman calls it "entrepreneurial medicine—we're transferring business concepts that are successful around the world and applying them to medicine."

Huntsman says this donation is only a beginning. When the money is spent, if a cure is not yet found, he will give

Jon Huntsman was an ensign in the Navy.

Jon Huntsman married Karen Haight as soon as he finished his studies at the University of Pennsylvania.

another $100 million, and another, if necessary.

With all his business success, it is Huntsman's family that gives him the greatest satisfaction. He says, "Karen and I met when we were 12 years of age. She has always been very much a part of anything I've done." Huntsman says he and Karen have built their lives around three main areas—their family, their business, and their faith. Finding a balance between the three is, he thinks, their secret of success. "Our family has always come first. To work with your children and still think of each other as friends takes a great deal of sensitivity, patience, love, and concern. It is a unique situation, and a great blessing." He adds, "We've always felt that a spiritual background and a positive set of values has helped us place the proper priorities on our family and our business. Our service to others is an integral part of anything we do."

Of his Horatio Alger Award, Huntsman says, "I am very humbled to receive this distinguished award. Many others are far more deserving." ◆

Jon Huntsman in his White House office.

The Huntsman family with then President Richard Nixon.

The Huntsman family in the Oval Office.

The Huntsman family.

JAMES EARL JONES

ACTOR

It could be said that James Earl Jones possesses the "voice of the century." Who in this country, or the world for that matter, is not familiar with this gifted actor's resonant sound? But what is not widely known about him is that as a child he was a stutterer who spent years unable to utter simple sentences. His journey toward finding his voice and ending the silence is what Jones says was much more important than the fame that followed.

Jones' parents, Robert Earl and Ruth Jones, were working and trying to make a life for themselves and their soon-to-be-born baby. They worked for a wealthy family in Memphis. Robert Earl was a chauffeur and butler, and Ruth was a maid. They lived above a garage, trying to save money for their own home. But Ruth was not content, and she left her husband before her son was born. She returned home to her parents, John Henry and Maggie Connolly, in Arkabatula, Mississippi, where Jones was born in 1931. Robert Earl Jones came to visit his son shortly after his birth, but after holding him for a moment and making his startled son cry, Robert Earl left. Jones did not see his father again for 21 years.

Ruth Jones became an occasional mother. Her times at home were fewer and farther between. Jones counted the days until she arrived for a visit. He recalls that "as soon as I saw her, I would go to the calendar and mark the day of her leave-taking. I rejoiced in her visits, yet her impending departure brought me to grief."

His home, then, was with his grandparents, and he began to think of them as his parents, calling them Papa and Mama. John Henry Connolly was the grandson of a slave and an Irish indentured servant. Twelve people lived in his four-room house, where Jones was born. They worked their own farm and sharecropped others. While it was not an easy life, it was one Jones enjoyed. He wrote in his autobiography, "I was blessed to grow up in the country. Even during the Depression and the war, there were certain advantages in being a farm family. You had healthy food when others were rationed. I was grounded in a work ethic determined by nature more than by man. The land gives you that sense of validation. It challenges you in a self-reliance."

Even as a child, Jones had a booming and noticeable voice. "My papa told me my voice was beautiful, like a bell," says Jones. He recalls how much he enjoyed sitting on the porch of his papa's house listening to the "music of Southern voices" telling stories and gossip. But by the time he was five, he also heard his grandparents planning for a move up north, which filled young Jones with dread.

In the early 1930s there were only four high schools for black children in the whole state of Mississippi. Students had to travel far and often board to get a high school education. It was important to John Henry that his children receive the best education possible, so he bought farmland sight unseen in Michigan, where he thought they would have more opportunities.

Jones remembers they carried packed meals on the train north. "We couldn't eat with the white passengers in the dining car," he recalls. They spent that winter in a converted chicken coop with rugs to cover the cold, concrete floor. The move proved to be a traumatic one for Jones. He became a stutterer, unable to speak at all in front of strangers. Jones remembers an uncle who was a stutterer and

whom Jones mocked. "After I started to stutter, I thought I was cursed for mocking my uncle." Jones is convinced that leaving Mississippi is what caused the problem. "When I was 40 I returned to the homestead for a reunion, and this warmth washed over me as I walked onto the property."

The early school years were difficult for young Jones. To avoid embarrassment over his

stuttered speech, his teachers tested him privately. In high school, it was a teacher who helped Jones find his voice. Jones wrote a poem for class, and the teacher made him read it out loud to him. "It broke something loose," Jones remembers. "The poetic rhythm is easier for the stutterer." From then on, Jones developed his new voice. By his senior year he was a class officer, editor of the

yearbook, and the school's champion public speaker. Jones won a scholarship to the University of Michigan.

In 1949, Jones entered the University of Michigan as a premed student. While his scholarship covered his tuition, he had to work for his expenses. He delivered the *Detroit Free Press* Sunday edition to dorm rooms, worked the switchboard, and even posed for art classes. He

joined the ROTC and began acting in school plays. After two years he decided he was not science-oriented. He dropped his premed courses and finished with a major in drama. "I had no intention of becoming an actor. I was a mason by trade, and I thought I'd go into construction. I just wasn't thinking far ahead."

After his tour with the Army, Jones decided to try his hand at acting. He did summer stock theatre near his home in Michigan and served as the stage electrician, carpenter, and manager. In his second year, he began doing bit parts and for a short time took a stage name: Todd Jones. Hoping to be a professional actor, he left for New York in the 1950s.

Jones was accepted into the American Theatre wing to study drama. Briefly, he lived with Robert Earl Jones. The pair did odd jobs, sometimes working together as janitors. "Robert Earl wanted the status of being my father, but I couldn't give him that," says Jones. He move out and lived in a cold water flat for $19 a month.

In the early 1960s, Jones starred in *The Blacks*, which had a three-year run. The play launched the careers of several actors including

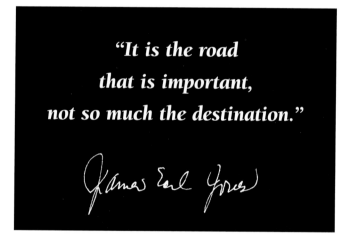

"It is the road that is important, not so much the destination."

James Earl Jones

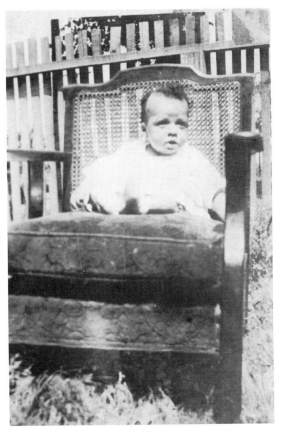

James Earl Jones as a baby in Mississippi.

James Earl Jones (left) with his cousin, his uncle, and his aunts.

Bill Dee Williams, Lou Gossett, Jr., Maya Angelou, and Cicely Tyson. In 1962, Jones won an Obie award as best actor in Off-Broadway theatre.

A year later, he made his debut in the movies with *Dr. Strangelove*, which was his last movie role for four years. Filled with self-doubt about his vocation, Jones went for testing to see where his talents lay. He was told he should be an architect. He enrolled in a design school, but an acting job came up and he got his career back on track.

In 1964, Jones played Othello for the third time. "I lived in Othello's skin most of that year," says Jones. "We were scheduled for 19 performances in Central Park, then moved to the Martinique Theatre in New York. We gave 224 performances there." Jones received the Drama Desk Award for best performance by an actor.

Jones' biggest chance came when he starred in *The Great White Hope*, the story of boxer Jack Johnson, the first black heavyweight champion. "I didn't know I could make a living at acting until this play," says Jones. He did both the

Jones' birthplace — Arkabutla, Mississippi.

stage and movie versions. Many said Jones was the perfect choice for the most powerful stage role of the decade. He won a Tony award for his performance, and two years later was nominated for an Oscar for the movie version.

Twenty years later, Jones got his second big stage role when he played Broadway as Troy Maxon in *Fences* in 1987. "An actor," says Jones, "is blessed if once in a lifetime lightning strikes him with a thunderbolt of a role. It is extraordinary if he is struck twice. This has happened to me with *The Great White Hope* in 1968 and then again with *Fences* in 1987." Jones' awards for this role include the Tony Award, Drama Desk Award, the Outer Critics Circle Award, and the Distinguished Performance Award from the Drama League of New York.

While he loved the theatre as his training arena, performing on stage night after night had become too demanding for Jones. He decided to give his full attention to Hollywood. Popular movie success came to Jones as the voice of

James Earl Jones in "The Great White Hope."

James Earl Jones in "Of Mice and Men."

Iowa farmer Ray Kinsella (Kevin Costner) enlists the help of reclusive author Terence Mann (James Earl Jones) in "Field of Dreams."

James Earl Jones in "Othello."

James Earl Jones in "Fences."

Darth Vader in the *Star Wars* trilogy. Since then he has starred in numerous movies including *Field of Dreams, The Hunt for Red October, Sneakers, Sommersby, The Sandlot, Cry the Beloved Country,* and *The Family Thing.*

Jones has won Emmy nominations for his roles in the George C. Scott series *East Side, West Side* and in HBO's *By Dawn's Early Light.* He also won two Emmys, as best actor in a drama series for *Gabriel's Fire* and as best supporting actor in a miniseries or special for the TNT movie *Heat Wave.*

Today, the voice of James Earl Jones is always in demand. He may be seen and heard more than any other actor in the world. "In the years of my silence," says Jones, "I was robbing myself of any presence. I am who I am. I was denying myself that." To the enjoyment of millions, Jones found his voice and went on to become what actor Sidney Poitier once called "a national treasure."

In his personal life, Jones finds solace and contentment. He and his wife Ceci, an actress who played Desdemona to Jones' Othello in 1981,

Robert Redford and James Earl Jones in "Sneakers."

and son Flynn live on a farm in upstate New York. In his autobiography, Jones writes, "The country cleanses my spirit and purges my body of the sounds, fumes, and toxins of urban life."

When asked what advice he would give others Jones uses a quote from Carl Sandburg, "Take not advice, including this." Jones does not believe in presenting himself as a role model, or someone who has all the answers. Instead, he believes it is the search, the learning, and the journey that are impor-tant. "The rehearsal part of a play is the best part," Jones explains. "No one sees it, and it's hard to share, but that's the cre-ative period. This is the road to. I think it is the road to that is important, not so much the destina-tion. The exciting part is getting there."

His Horatio Alger Award is a signpost that he has reached at least one destination—he is a successful, highly acclaimed actor. "It is an honor to receive this award," he says. "It means a great deal to me to be included in such a distin-guished membership." ◆

James Earl Jones with former President and Mrs. George Bush.

James Earl Jones with his wife Ceci and son Flynn.

James Earl Jones after a speech with President and Mrs. Bill Clinton and Vice President and Mrs. Al Gore.

PATRICK C. KELLY

CHAIRMAN AND CEO
PHYSICIAN SALES & SERVICE, INC.

Patrick Kelly holds the record at the Virginia Home for Boys as the youngest child to live at the orphanage. He also has the distinction of being the home's longest resident. While many would be reticent about revealing these "achievements," Kelly is honored to share his experiences at the home because in his heart that is where his parents lived, and it is where he learned values that have served him well throughout his life.

Kelly's father deserted the family in 1947, when his wife was still preg-nant with their son. Kelly was the family's third child; he has an older brother and sister. His mother struggled to raise her children on her own, but eventually began having to leave her boys with relatives. After five years of being passed around to different aunts and uncles, Kelly was taken to the Virginia Home for Boys in Rich-mond, where his brother was already in residence.

"The rule of the home was that you had to be eight to live there, but my mother appealed to the minister of our church and they made an exception for me," explains Kelly. So, at the tender age of five, Kelly became a member of a fraternity that would have lasting effects on his character and point of view.

The couple who were guardians of the home, Mr. and Mrs. John Woods, became the lov-ing "parents" Kelly had always craved. "Pop Woods," recalls Kelly, "was responsible for maintenance and disci-pline in the home. Mrs. Woods ran the books and kitchen. There were 40 boys living there at the time and I was the youngest. They babied me." Still, the boys each had duties and clear expectations. "I did housekeeping jobs because I was the small-est." In addition, the boys had to keep their dormitory rooms clean, help in the kitchen, and work in the garden, where they raised their own vegetables.

In addition to having the first real structure and routine in his life,

Kelly learned other values from Pop Woods. "He taught team building," says Kelly. "We had to work together to make the home a success. When more than 40 people live under one roof, you have to be a team to make it work."

Kelly also remembers a time when he stole a tube of glue from a store in Richmond. "I was eight years old and needed some glue to put together an airplane model I received as a gift at Christmas. I didn't have any money to buy glue, so I tried to steal it from the five and dime in town. The manager of the store caught me and called the police, who in turn called Pop. We drove back to the home in silence in Pop's '52 Ford. We stopped in front of the home and he turned to me and said, 'Pat do you know what you did?' I said, 'Yes, Mr. Woods.' He said, 'You're too smart a boy to do this. I trust you not to do this again. Now get out.' So, he didn't beat me, which is what I expected. He talked to me. Today, we have a credo in our company: It's easier to ask for forgiveness than permission. I encourage people to make mistakes because it's easier to say I'm sorry. We don't punish people for making mistakes. That comes

from the way Pop treated me. I never stole again."

Two years later, after 30 years of directing the home, Mr. and Mrs. Woods retired. Kelly was not so lucky with the home's new guardian. "He was a strong disciplinarian," remembers Kelly. "He beat me when I made mistakes. That's why today I tell people who work for me that making mistakes won't ruin their career."

When Kelly was 14, the home got a new director, Bill Hazelgrove. "He was loving and kept me out of trouble," says Kelly. Kelly was a bright student and earned his way by working full time, but he began running around with a gang. He picked fights, and could have followed a self-defeating path. Instead, Kelly credits Hazelgrove with keeping him straight.

Kelly recalls a time when he was 14. He was walking on the grounds of the home when a taxi

pulled up. The driver asked if he knew Pat Kelly. "That's me," said Kelly. "I'm your father," said the driver. It was a shock for young Kelly. His father invited him to come and spend a weekend with his second wife and family. Kelly did so, but a relationship was not established. He never saw his father again until the week before he died as an elderly man.

The relationships Kelly developed at the home were far more important to him. His brother was adopted just two years after Kelly arrived, so he reached out to his 39 other brothers for camaraderie. Today, Kelly says, "I'm glad I was raised at the home. At first I thought, 'What's wrong with me?' But when I talk to the boys who live in that home today, I tell them it is not what's wrong with them, it's what's wrong with their parents. As soon you

realize that, you can get on with our life and the world of opportunities ahead of you."

Kelly did just that. To earn money as a youth, Kelly worked full time in the kitchen after he was 12; a job that earned him $5 a week. When he was 15, he worked at a drug store. Then, at 16, he worked for Safeway full time until he was 18, going to school during the day and working nights.

Kelly took what he earned in high school and entered the Virginia Commonwealth University. While he had always been a bright student, he wasn't used to applying himself to his studies. After his first semester, he failed all but one class. "It was my first real freedom and I just played," explains Kelly. The year was 1966, and, without a student deferment, Kelly was drafted into the Army.

Kelly married while in the service, and then spent a year in Vietnam. When he returned, he went to see the dean at Virginia Commonwealth to see if he could get back into school under the GI Bill. After he was refused, Kelly made a deal with the dean. "I told him, 'If I don't have straight Bs in six months, I will quit and you won't have to kick me out.' The dean accepted my offer. I got straight As,

> *"Commit to making something of yourself, and success will come."*
>
> Patrick Kelly

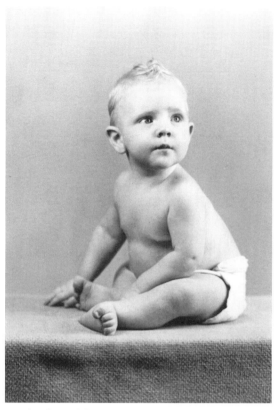

Patrick Kelly as a baby.

and went on to earn a four-year premed degree in under three years."

When Kelly graduated, his wife was pregnant, and he decided that it would be best to work rather than go on to medical school. He taught school for six months, realized that wasn't what he wanted to do, and then took a job with General Medical, a medical supply company in Richmond. That job sent him to Atlanta, where he excelled in sales. When his boss went to a competitor in Texas, Intermedco, Kelly went with him. Later he took over the sales territory in Jacksonville, Florida, where he was so successful, Intermedco offered him a vice presidency in 1982. When the company was sold to a British firm, the new owners were not interested in the physician market, which Kelly had developed so successfully. He was given his walking papers in 1983.

Kelly returned to Jacksonville and formed a partnership with three

Patrick Kelly with his mother.

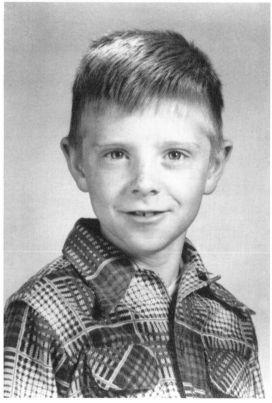

Patrick Kelly at age 7.

Patrick C. Kelly

friends. Each mortgaged their home and took out loans to get their company, Physician Sales and Service, Inc. (PSS), started. They offered local physicians next-day delivery of any common item—something their competitors could not match. Eventually, Kelly developed computer systems and his own fleet of delivery trucks to keep his business competitive.

Today, PSS is the largest distributor of medical supplies, equipment, and pharmaceuticals to primary care and other office-based physicians. PSS operates 62 service centers and has become an international company operating with a subsidiary known as WorldMed, Inc., to reach European doctors and hospitals. The company has grown 40 percent every year since it started in 1983. Recently, Kelly also started Diagnostic Imaging, a national X-ray distributor. "We believe we can grow into a worldwide health care distributor."

SLUGGER—Pat Kelly, the youngest boy ever admitted to the Richmond Home for Boys, swings during a softball game that was part of a celebration of the 107th anniversary of the home yesterday. The catcher is Arthur C. Sanders, president-elect of the Optimist Club, and Durwood Sims, an alumnus of the home, is the umpire.

Pat Kelly playing baseball at the Richmond Home for Boys' 107th Anniversary.

THE RICHMOND NEWS LEADER
SATURDAY, JUNE 18, 1955

Pat Kelly Has a Chat With Mr. and Mrs. John G. Wood at Boys' Home

PARENTS TO 500

TWO NOTE 26TH YEAR AT HOME FOR BOYS

By JOHN CONNORS

John and Bessie Wood are mother and father to more than 500 boys and men.

"And we're grandmother and grand-daddy many times over that," said Mrs. Wood.

The two are co-superintendents at the Richmond Home for Boys, observing its 109th anniversary today. It's an anniversary for the Woods too. They came to the home 26 years ago.

Pat Kelly with Mr. and Mrs. John G. Wood.

6 Richmond Times-Dispatch, Monday, March 18, 1957

Earth Is Turned For Boys' Home

By David M. Clinger

It was St. Patrick's Day and luck was with 10-year-old Pat Kelly.

When lots were drawn yesterday afternoon it was he who won the honor of breaking the first ground for the new Richmond Home for Boys on Broad street rd.

However, even though it was his lucky day, he still found that ground breaking can be a tough job. But while it was a struggle for him at first to sink the shovel into the ground, he finally managed to turn over a good-sized chunk of earth.

Home President Speaks

Main speaker for the event was E. Tucker Carlton, president of the home. He said he was "proud of the history of the home and the many fine boys who have been cared for and brought up there.

"We hope and expect to care for many more boys who are in need of such a home as ours throughout the next century and even thereafter."

He told how the plight of a homeless boy in 1846 had sparked the movement which established the home that year in the area between Church Hill and Union Hill. He traced the home's history, including its moves in 1854 to a building at St. James and Baker sts. and in 1870 to its present location at Amelia and Meadow sts.

Others participating in the program included Rayee Norris, vice president of the home, the Rev. Dr. Theodore F. Adams, Bobby Burns, a resident at the home, Augustus Schultz, the home's oldest living alumnus, P. C. Abbott, who directed the fund raising drive for the new home, and the quartet from Tabernacle Baptist Church.

Praises Home, Officers

Dr. Adams praised the home for its work in producing "good Christian, usable men," and

praised the officers of the home for "giving of themselves and of their substance in support of the work."

Honored at the ceremony were Mr. and Mrs. Bruce Dunstan who donated the 24-acre tract for the home. The land is located north of Broad street rd. just west of Skipwith.

The new home will consist of four cottages, each housing 12 boys, an administration building and a home for the superintendent. Construction is expected to start within several weeks.

Pat Kelly Breaks Ground for New Home for Boys Here
Home Site Is on Broad Street Rd. West of Skipwith

Pat Kelly breaking ground for the new Richmond Home for Boys.

Kelly served in Vietnam.

From the start, PSS was an employee-owned company. In fact, Kelly boasts that more than 150 employees are millionaires because of their vested interest in PSS. "It all goes back to the Virginia Home for Boys," says Kelly. "We shared everything—our marbles, our clothes, all of it. It was always 'we,' never 'I.' It was 'we will,' and 'we can.' I've built an organization around that."

In 1994, PSS went public and the company's share price has roughly quadrupled since then.

Kelly says the company succeeds due to the way in which employees are developed and trained. He says he expects his people not just to work hard, but to understand the business. Trainees, for example, undergo six months of learning the business from the bottom up. They spend weeks stocking inventory, driving trucks, emptying trash, and sweeping floors in the warehouse. "This ensures that every employee has empathy for everyone else," he says.

The current Richmond Home for Boys.

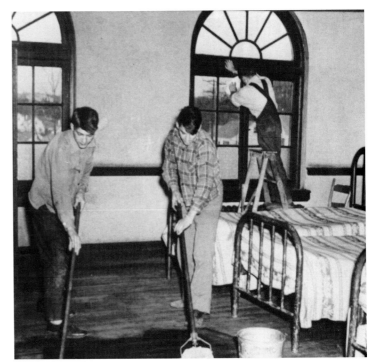
Keeping the dormitory spotless was the responsibility of each boy.

The Depression was on and Scott remembers playing kick-the-can and making up games that everyone could enjoy, but that didn't cost anything. He started working at an early age, even shoveling snow for neighbors when he was only eight. "Once, as I was shoveling the driveway for a neighbor, I dreamed during my hours of labor of making the grand sum of $1.50. My customer gave me 25 cents for my efforts. I learned from then on I would settle on what my contract was worth at the front end of the job," laughs Scott.

When he was older, Scott worked summers on farms and ranches doing a number of odd jobs, such as detasseling corn and taking care of livestock. One summer he hopped a train and worked on a ranch in Oregon. He enjoyed the agricultural life and had thought he would major in range management when he entered Colorado A&M, but a friend convinced him to take engineering. "If nothing else," he told Scott, "it teaches you to think logically." Scott reasoned that a skill such as that could transfer to many jobs, so he earned a degree in civil engineering. During college summers he worked for Kiewit, and

spent one summer working on a survey crew in North Dakota as a stake chaser and water boy.

When he was a senior in college, Scott married Carolyn Falk. She worked while Scott finished school. Upon graduation, Scott got a job with Kiewit as an engineer on a building in Omaha. The year was 1953, and Scott was soon called to serve during the Korean War. "I never got farther than Orlando,

Florida," he says. Scott worked as an Air Force installation officer, responsible for upkeep of the base. He was there for two years, then returned to Kiewit.

His first assignment was building a dam in California. The nation was in the midst of a major construction boom in the 1950s and 1960s, and Scott had to move his family to 17 job sites in 12 years. Scott was methodically working his

way up the ladder from foreman to job superintendent to district manager, crisscrossing the country from project to project. Housing was not always available when a job was in a remote area. Scott recalls that he once had to house his wife and two children in an apartment above a neighborhood tavern. Another time, they had to rent rooms in someone's home and live with strangers.

A firm believer in setting goals, Scott was living this nomadic life to get enough background and backing so that he could start a business of his own. "Several times," says Scott, "I came close to accomplishing what I thought I needed to start my own business. That's when Peter Kiewit would come along and give me a new challenge, a new opportunity, a new perspective. He was not aware of my desire to

leave to start my own business, and I never shared that with him in later years."

Kiewit became Scott's mentor. "To a great extent anything I know about business I learned from him," he says. He would describe his mentor as hard working, demanding, exacting, and not always pleasant to work for. On the other hand, Scott had a lot of respect for him. Much as Scott's mother did, Kiewit handed out one-liners that for Scott always made sense of a situation. One he remembers is, "If you're not sure whether something is right or wrong, consider whether you'd want to see it reported in the morning paper."

About a year before Kiewit died, he asked Scott if he thought he could run the company. Scott told him he could, but emphasized that because they were different people, he would not run the business the same way Kiewit had. Kiewit chose Walter Scott, Jr. as his successor.

When Scott became CEO of Kiewit in 1979, it was principally a construction business with some mining interests. Under his leadership, those businesses have prospered and Kiewit is currently considered one of the leading heavy con-

> ## *"Set goals for yourself. You should always have an objective you are trying to reach."*
>
> *Walter Scott*

Walter Scott as a toddler.

Walter Scott, age 11.

Walter Scott as an Eagle Scout.

Walter Scott hunting with his father Walter Sr.

Walter Scott as a young man.

Ready for an F-16 ride with the USAF Thunderbirds.

struction organizations in the nation. Projects range from a $40,000 paving job to the $750 million San Joaquin Hills toll road in Southern California. In addition, Scott has led the company into new ventures in telecommunications, energy, and investments in infrastructure projects.

While the company has retained its roots in construction, it has ventured into businesses on the cutting edge of new technologies. No one has benefited from these calculated risks more than Kiewit employees. From

Walter Scott (upper right) on his first Kiewit project after college.

Walter Scott is chairman of the Henry Doorly Zoo.

Walter Scott and his wife Suzanne.

Walter Scott with his family.

the beginning, Kiewit has been a privately held company whose stockholders are mostly employees. In fact, each of 300 employees owns stock in Kiewit worth at least $1 million.

Personal tragedy struck shortly after Scott became chairman of Kiewit. His wife Carolyn was diagnosed with cancer and after an extended illness died in 1983. "Obviously, that was a rough time for me," says Scott. He and Carolyn were married for 33 years and had four children.

In 1987, Scott remarried and today he and his wife Suzanne enjoy giving to their community—Omaha. Major contributions include the Scott Family Cat Complex and the Walter and Suzanne Scott Kingdoms of the Seas Aquarium at the Henry Doorly Zoo. "I have always told my children," says Scott, "that the greatest thing you can have in life is your good health. The greatest thing you can acquire in life is a good education. And the greatest thing you can do in life is to be a giver, because the world already has plenty of takers."

In addition, Scott advises young people to develop the habit of setting goals. "You should always have an objective you are trying to reach," he says. "Peter Kiewit used to say he was pleased, but not satisfied. I like the idea in that statement. Being pleased means you've done a good job, being satisfied means you don't have to do anything more. I'm never completely satisfied."

Of his Horatio Alger Award, this quiet leader says, "It's nice to know someone thinks I've done a reasonably good job." ◆

Walter Scott with prize marlin in Mexico.

Walter Scott deep sea fishing.

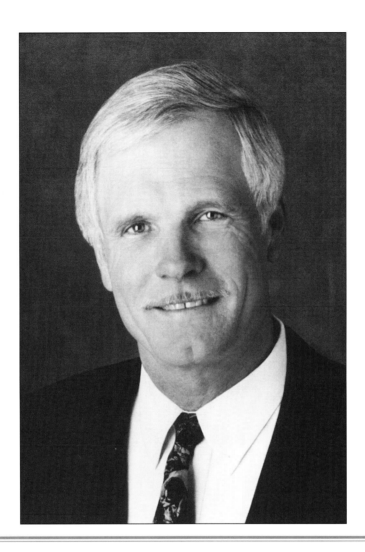

R. E. "TED" TURNER

VICE CHAIRMAN
TIME WARNER INC.

When Ted Turner became an account executive for Turner Advertising in 1960, it's unlikely he knew he would turn his family's billboard business into a communications giant known the world over. But he did know this— whatever he did in life, he'd do his best to be successful at it.

Born in 1938 in Cincinnati, Ohio, Turner was the son of Ed and Florence Turner. Turner's father worked for an outdoor advertising company after the family farm was lost during the Depression.

His goal was to one day own his own business. In 1939, his dream came true when he opened Turner Advertising.

When the United States entered World War II, Ed Turner joined the Navy. After learning he would be stationed on the Gulf Coast, he

and Florence decided to take their three-year-old daughter Mary Jean with them, but leave Turner in a school in Cincinnati. "It was scary for me to be on my own at such an early age," says Turner, "but my father wanted me to have a good education."

A year after the war ended, the Turners returned to Cincinnati and Ted was placed in a public school. Turner Advertising began to do well and Ed Turner expanded the business, buying two billboard companies in Savannah. He moved the family to Georgia. Soon after they arrived, Ted was sent to military school in Chattanooga. He was the only seventh-grade boarder at the school.

While Ted wasn't anxious to attend the school, he learned to love it and its discipline. There was a strict code of ethics there—no lying, cheating, or stealing. Ted was said to be extremely honest, even owning up to childish pranks he occasionally played. It was also at this time that a beloved Bible teacher had an influence on him. Young Turner became religious and even considered becoming a missionary. But his faith was shaken when in 1953 his sister Mary Jean became ill with a painful, deadly case of lupus. Her long illness put a strain on the family. Turner's parents divorced in 1957, and his sister died five years after the onset of her illness when she was only 17.

From the time he was 12, Turner worked for his father. During the summer, he worked 40 hours a week doing hard manual labor for the company. He made $20 a week, but his father required him to pay room and board. He also required his son to read two books a week. "I never thought not to do as I was told," says Turner. The alternative was a physical reprimand. Turner explains his father's harsh treatment by saying, "He just did what he thought he had to do to raise me to be a strong, competitive man."

Turner graduated from high school in 1956, and was named best sailor and debater. He entered Brown University and majored in Greek classics. His father did not approve of his choice, however, and Ted later changed his major to economics.

In 1960, Turner left Brown, where he was vice president of the Debating Union and Commodore of the Yacht Club. He spent the summer with the Coast Guard, then went to work as an account executive for Turner Advertising. By

1962, the company was doing well and had become the biggest billboard business in the South. Unfortunately, Ed Turner was not doing as well. He was depressed, and many thought he just needed a vacation. It came as a shock to everyone when he committed suicide in 1963. Turner says of this difficult time, "My father's death was devastating to me. With his death I lost my idol and my teacher."

Another shock came quickly after Ed Turner's funeral, when Ted discovered his father had sold Turner Advertising. The new owners offered Turner a chance to buy back the business for $200,000 cash, which he did not have. He took them up on their offer, but instead of paying them he convinced them to take stock in the company. Turner became president and chief operating officer, and by 1970 Turner

Advertising was a multi-million dollar business.

Against all advice, Turner bought a bankrupt UHF station, channel 17 in Atlanta. The station was a bottomless pit of financial need. "All the money we made in the billboard business was poured into the TV station," says Turner. An idea occurred to him to buy inexpensive programming, such as syndicated re-runs and movies, and price them

"All my life
I've done things others said
couldn't be done."

for a local market. At the same time, he boosted advertising prices by expanding his range. He broadcasted on a microwave dish, reaching viewers in five states. Within 18 months, the station began to show a profit.

In the mid-1970s Turner knew he needed new programming for channel 17. He thought sports would provide hours of free programming if he owned the

team. In 1976, he bought the Atlanta Braves baseball team and, a year later, he entered a limited partnership with the Atlanta Hawks basketball team. Local fans had to watch channel 17 to see the games.

Turner's real genius came about with the use of communication satellites. Once he learned that a small station could reach a much bigger audience with the use of satellites, he made channel 17 (now known as TBS Superstation) a national station in a single stroke. In fact, channel 17 was the first superstation broadcast via satellite to cable systems nationwide. Quickly, the Hawks and Braves gained fans all over the country.

In 1977, Turner entered the America's Cup race as skipper of *Courageous*. He won the trials in a tremendous come-from-behind race. As defender for the United States, Turner won a clean sweep—all four races. The media dubbed him "Captain Outrageous."

Turner's next challenge came in 1980 when he bet everything on his vision for the future of broadcasting. He created a 24-hour cable news network and called it CNN. Critics said no one would watch so much news, but

Ted Turner as a boy.

Ted Turner's mother Florence.

Ted Turner's father Ed.

Turner was confident it would work. In its first year, CNN lost more than $2 million a month, but Turner continued to expand. He launched CNN Headline News and CNN International, as well as CNN Radio. He also produced documentaries on issues such as pollution, hunger, and the arms race.

Five years later, Turner realized he had to go to the next level with his business. He explains, "I'm in the communications business. You don't want to fight the next war with the last war's weapons. I had to get stronger in distribution or programming. I knew I wasn't strong enough to withstand a long, protracted war with the networks. I had to go to another level to be able to compete. I'd gotten a jump with CNN, but I was still much smaller than the networks. They were 20 or 30 times bigger than me. I could see I was going to lose, and I didn't want that to happen."

He made a bid to buy CBS. "It was like a kid at the lemonade stand trying to buy the local supermarket," says Turner. "We were a $100 million company trying to make a $2 billion acquisition." When the deal with CBS didn't work out, Turner acquired MGM for $1.4 billion.

In 1985, Turner founded the Goodwill Games in an attempt to provide worldwide sports competition free from political pressures, and to promote peace and mutual understanding through sport. The first Games were held in Moscow in 1986, and have been held every four years since then.

Turner Broadcasting sold portions of MGM, but retained the MGM library of film and television properties. This library formed the initial programming cornerstone of TNT. Launched in 1988, it debuted with *Gone With the Wind*, one of Turner's favorite movies in the library.

In 1989, CNN became a household name. It showed Tianamen Square as it happened, as well as the fall of the Berlin Wall and the U.S. invasion of Panama. Turner Broadcasting stock was quintupling and showing record profits. Turner was named by *Forbes* as one of the 400 richest men in America.

The next two years were good ones for Ted Turner. He met actress, activist, and businesswoman Jane Fonda. They married in 1991, and Turner, who had been married two times previously, says, "This is my last marriage." Of all the people who have had an influence on Turner, he

Ted Turner in Cincinnati, Ohio.

Ted Turner and his sister Mary Jean.

Ted Turner with neighborhood children.

81

Ted Turner in the Navy.

Ted Turner in uniform.

Ted Turner with his Naval unit.

says Fonda has had a "tremendous positive impact." This was also the year the Atlanta Braves would go from worst to first, and Ted Turner was named Man of the Year by *Time* magazine. He was 53, the age his father was when he died. At the time, Turner said of his father, "If I had one wish, it would be to bring him back and show him around."

Turner Broadcasting continued to expand, acquiring the entertainment assets of Hanna-Barbera Cartoons. In 1994, TBS launched the Cartoon Network, the world's first 24-hour, all-animation service. Castle Rock Entertainment joined the company in 1993. Movies produced with this group include *In the Line of Fire, When Harry Met Sally, City Slickers, The Shawshank Redemption,* and *The American President,* as well as the television series *Seinfeld.*

In 1994, Turner Broadcasting merged with New Line Cinema, the leading independent producer and distributor of motion pictures. Turner also oversees Turner Pictures, which recently released its first film, *Michael.*

The following year, CNNfn was launched, offering 14 hours of financial news. It was another first.

Turner Broadcasting was bought in 1996 by Time Warner Inc. for $7.5 billion. Today, Turner serves as Time Warner's vice chairman. In addition to his duties with Time Warner, Turner is an avid environmentalist. He devotes himself to saving the planet. "What we do to the environment, we do to ourselves," he says. "But there is reason for hope. The Cold War is over. We saved the whales and bald eagles. The gray wolf is back in Yellowstone. One hundred years ago we were taking three steps backward with our environment. Now we are taking one step forward and two backward. Maybe in another 50 years, we'll take two steps forward."

Turner founded the Turner Foundation Inc., the family's private grant-making organization, which focuses on population and the environment. He hopes to endow the foundation with $500 million.

When asked if he thinks his efforts to save the environment will be successful, Turner says, "All my life I've done things others said couldn't be done. Can we save the world? I think so. I'm going to do everything I can to make it happen." ◆

Ted Turner as a young businessman.

Ted Turner as he launched CNN.

Ted Turner as captain of the Courageous.

Opportunity

1997
Horatio Alger
National
Scholars

ALABAMA

Shauna Dallas
Le Flore High School of Communications and Arts, Mobile, Alabama

"I don't think of obstacles as hardships; they are instead God's way of building self-reliant character," says Shauna, whose goal is to be first in her class in academics. Ranked in the top five percent, Shauna is a Principal's Scholar at her school. She has been active in student government, Key Club, French Club, Science Olympics, and National Honor Society. She also served for two years as treasurer of the African American Club. Shauna is an active volunteer in her church, and has even served as a singer at church-related

functions. She also spends time taking care of family members. Shauna plans to attend Howard University and major in biomedical engineering. Receiving the best education possible is her most immediate goal.

ALABAMA

Stephanie Rush
Fairhope High School, Fairhope, Alabama

An active member of the Junior ROTC program in her school, Stephanie holds the position of cadet executive officer, which places her second in command of the entire unit. Involvement in NJROTC has allowed Stephanie to practice and develop her leadership skills. Her involvement in the program has included the NJROTC Academic Team, Exhibition Drill Team, Regulation Drill Team, and Rifle Team. Stephanie has received medals for Outstanding Leadership from the Veterans of Foreign Wars as well as the Retired Officers Association. She has also been an active member of French

Club. She works 20 hours a week during the school year, and increases that to full time in the summer. Stephanie hopes to attend the University of Alabama and major in business management. "One day I would like to start my own business," she says.

ALASKA

Summer Kuth
Tok High School, Tok, Alaska

"Without the experiences I've had in my life, I would not be the person I am today," says Summer, a member of the National Honor Society and her school's honor roll. She is ranked first in her class. Active in basketball, Summer has participated in state tournaments. She once won second place in a speech contest sponsored by the Veterans of Foreign Wars. For the last five years, Summer has worked full time in the summer. She plans to attend the University of Alaska at Anchorage, where she will

major in elementary education, or possibly special education. A responsible young woman, Summer says, "I am looking forward to learning and bettering my life, as well as the lives of others."

ARIZONA

Sarah Lewis
Yuma High School, Yuma, Arizona

Ranked first in her class, Sarah is a member of National Honor Society, and a long-time member of her school's A-Team Honor Roll. She is active in Thespian Club, where she serves as treasurer, and Interact Club, of which she is the president and finance chairperson. She has also served as the vice president and secretary of Discovery Club. Sarah participates in American Field Service, Young Republicans, and Dance Club. An active volunteer, Sarah spends time with Senior Olympics and the Rotary Club. She plans to attend

Northern Arizona University in Flagstaff. She hopes to pursue a career in the medical field, and possibly genetic research. She says, "I want to work in field where I can help people and make a difference in their future."

ARIZONA

James Phair III
Chandler High School, Chandler, Arizona

An excellent swimmer, James made the varsity swim team when he was in the ninth grade. Since then, he has participated in regional and state competitions. He serves as parliamentarian in Vocational Industrial Clubs of America as well as for the Arizona Regional Youth Council. He has served as vice president for the Christian Youth Fellowship, and was chaplain for the Easter Pilgrimage. He won the citizenship award from the American Legion, and has received the team scholar athlete award from his school. James volunteers much of his time to church-related programs and says that he may one day be interested in a ministry to youth. For now, he hopes to attend Chapman University in Orange, California. He plans to combine his interest in electronics with a degree in education.

ARKANSAS

Curt Evans
Crossett High School, Crossett, Arkansas

Ranked first in his class, Curt is president of National Honor Society as well as Mu Alpha Theta. He has also served as vice president of Foreign Language Honor Society. Curt is active with National Beta Club, Science Club, Students for Christ, Quiz Bowl, and football. He has received awards for biology and perfect attendance, and was named Student Athlete by the National College Football Hall of Fame. He also received the Arkansas Governor's School Award, sponsored by the Arkansas Department of Education. Curt works full time each summer, but during the school year he volunteers with Vision 2000 and Adopt a Grandparent. He plans to attend the University of Arkansas in Fayetteville, and major in engineering or pre-medicine. He says, "Being able to focus on my school work has been very helpful."

ARKANSAS

Karen Newcom
Marion High School, Marion, Arkansas

A hard-working student, Karen is involved with Junior Achievement. She has also participated in French Club, Pride, and student council. Karen enjoys volunteer work, has spent time working on a community festival, and has served as a stage hand for a community play. She works part time in a clinic, which gives her practical experience for her career goal to be a registered nurse. She hopes to attend the Methodist Hospital School of Nursing in Memphis. After she earns her degree, Karen says she wants to work in a doctor's office. "I want to work directly with patients. I love to meet people and make them feel comfortable."

CALIFORNIA

Guadalupe Lara
Woodlake High School, Woodlake, California

Taking challenging courses that will prepare her for college, Guadalupe has maintained a straight-A average throughout her high school career. In addition to being ranked in the top five percent of her class, Guadalupe has received awards for business, math, and perfect attendance. She is active in Maya Club, Ecology Club, Science Club, California State Federation, and Dance Club. Fluent in Spanish, Guadalupe serves as a translator during parent-teacher conferences. She works part time during the school year, and full time during the summer. She plans to attend the University of California at Riverside and major in business administration. "I will be the first member of my large family to attend college. I want to serve as a positive role model to my younger siblings."

CALIFORNIA

Miguel Angel Lopez
Healdsburg High School, Healdsburg, California

Ranked in the top 10 percent of his class, Miguel works hard to maintain high academic standards. He has received awards in algebra and geometry. He is a member of Mesa Club and College Bound. Miguel volunteers as a tutor, and even teaches a sixth-grade class for one hour each week. He works full time each summer, saving money for college. He hopes to attend California Polytechnic, San Luis Obispo. He plans to major in mechanical engineering. He says, "My parents are wise mentors to me. I will be the first member of my family to go to college. It's something I want to do for my family. All my hard work is paying off as I reach my goal of getting a college education."

COLORADO

Mandy Forssberg
Las Animas High School, Las Animas, Colorado

Ranked number one in her class, Mandy is a member of the National Honor Society. Recently, she was named National Scholar by the Congressional Youth Leadership Council. She is active in Science Olympiad, Mock Trial, Future Business Leaders of America, and Knowledge Bowl. She also enjoys participating in school plays. Mandy has volunteered as a Boys and Girls Club tutor, and has worked several part-time jobs. She has logged in a number of hours babysitting, and she hopes to one day own her own day care center. She is planning to major in business management and minor in early childhood education at Colorado State University at Fort Collins. She says, "Getting a college education is the next step that will improve my life."

COLORADO

Mary Grace Legg
Abraham Lincoln High School, Denver, Colorado

An avid student, Mary Grace is ranked near the top of her class. She has received awards for outstanding achievement, the honor roll, the State Senator Award, and the AEAC Student Award from the Asian Education Advisory. She is active in MESA (math engineering), Octagon Cub, National Honor Society, Drama Club, Renaissance Guild, and marching band. She enjoys doing volunteer work with her church, as well as the Filipino-American Community of Colorado. In addition, she has a part-time job in an office. Mary Grace hopes to attend the University of Colorado at Boulder. She plans to major in medicine. "I want to be a pediatrician either in a private practice or in the emergency care unit of a hospital," she says. A talented high school actress, Mary Grace will minor in performing arts.

CONNECTICUT

Kenya Jackson
Manchester High School, Manchester, Connecticut

A long-time member of student council, Kenya is a former vice president of her class. She has worked extensively for her school's Human Relations Council, and has served as a peer mediator. She is also involved in Drill Team and Multicultural Club. She has participated in the Connecticut State Leadership Camp, and volunteers for the Office of Student Activities. She works nearly full time throughout the year. Kenya plans to attend Morgan State College in Baltimore, Maryland. She wants to major in accounting to prepare herself to become a certified public accountant. She says, "I want to get a college degree not only for myself, but for my mother who has always been a positive role model for me."

CONNECTICUT

Jennifer Ng'andu
New London High School, New London, Connecticut

A hard-working student at the top of her class, Jennifer serves as treasurer of National Honor Society. She is also president of her class, co-editor of the yearbook, and captain of the cheerleading squad. She participates in Drama Team, Math Team, Peer Mediation, and the New London Scholars Program. She has received awards in Spanish, English, history, and art. Last year, she was named the Rotary Scholar of the Year. Jennifer also actively volunteers for her church youth group, Phone-a-Teen, and Key Club. She hopes to attend Yale University and major in pre-medicine. She says, "I would like to have a career in surgery or neurology. I would also like to travel around the world and experience different cultures."

DELAWARE

Cheryl Fischer
Dover High School, Dover, Delaware

Cheryl has worked hard to maintain a high grade point average. She is a member of National Honor Society and Science Olympiad. She is president of Environmental Club, treasurer of English Club, and has served as president of German Club. She sings in the women's chorus as well as the gospel chorus. Cheryl is also a member of ROTC, and is currently on the rifle team. She has received the Gold Award in Girl Scouts. Her volunteer work includes Special Olympics and HOPE—Helping Other People's Environments. Cheryl hopes to attend Randolph-Macon Woman's College in Virginia. She wants to major in biology. "My ultimate goal," she says "is to do research on the physical and chemical aspects of emotional stability."

DELAWARE

Jonathan Gibson
Sussex Central High School, Georgetown, Delaware

"I like to be a leader in the classroom by setting a good example, assuming an active role, and initiating lively debates," says Jonathan, who is ranked in the top 10 percent of his class. He has been on the high honor roll throughout his high school career, and was named Outstanding Scholar at his school. He has served as president or RPG, a role playing club, and as vice president of the literary magazine. He is also active in Foreign Language Club and drama. Jonathan has participated in a library program reading to children, and has coached Little League baseball. He also works at a part-time job throughout the year. He plans to attend the University of Delaware in Newark and major in criminal justice.

DISTRICT OF COLUMBIA

Cristina Berrios
Francis L. Cardozo Sr. High School, Washington, D.C.

Coming to the United States when she was an adolescent, Cristina had to work hard to learn English. She accomplished that goal on her own, and is now ranked in the top 10 percent of her class. She is a member of National Honor Society, and has participated in Model United Nations, Saturday Academy, and TransTech Academy. She has also participated in Junior ROTC. Cristina has volunteered her time in a reading program and a workshop called It's US. She hopes to attend Elmira College in New York, or George Washington University. Her goal is to be a pediatrician. If necessary, she will train as a nurse so that she can work her way through medical school. She says, "I would like to show other foreign students that there is nothing too difficult to accomplish if they want to do it."

DISTRICT OF COLUMBIA

Theresa McCoy

Eastern Sr. High School, Washington, D.C.

Currently, music is a big part of Theresa's life. She is a member of the marching band, concert band, and jazz ensemble. Ranked in the top five percent of her class, Theresa has received awards in English, math, and history. She has participated in Tri-M Music Honor Society and the school newspaper. She does volunteer work with her church, and has a part-time job. She plans to attend Georgetown University or Howard University. Theresa wants to major in pre-medicine and minor in music education. She says, "I would like to have my own doctor's office and music school. I think these goals are attainable. I have a plan in life. I will never let go of my dreams."

FLORIDA

Heidi Alexa

St. Cloud High School, St. Cloud, Florida

Ranked first in her class, Heidi is her school's Junior Achievement representative. A member of National Honor Society, Heidi also participates in Mu Alpha Theta, Chemistry/Physics Club, Biology Club, Keyettes, and Wrestlerettes. She is planning to attend college, but has not yet decided where she will go.

FLORIDA

Katherine Larimore

Osceola High School, Kissimmee, Florida

A former secretary of National Honor Society, Kate is ranked in the top five percent of her class. Recently, she was named Osceolan of the Year in her school yearbook in recognition of her academic achievements. She has participated in chorus and the Homecoming Committee. In addition, Kate received a blue ribbon for Best Speech sponsored by Toastmasters International. She plans to attend Clearwater Christian College in Clearwater, Florida. She will major in English and journalism and minor in history. She says, "I hope to become an English teacher of middle level or senior high school students. It is my desire to inspire my students to reach for the highest goals possible, and to perform well in life no matter what obstacles they might encounter along the way."

GEORGIA

Yvonne Reid

Harlem Comprehensive High School, Harlem, Georgia

A strong student, Yvonne is a member of National Honor Society, Beta Club, and Spanish Honor Society. She also participates in Future Homemakers of America. Yvonne was once in Junior ROTC, where she received a Best Platoon Leader award. She has also participated in track and field. Yvonne works full time throughout the school year. Her plan for the future includes attending Augusta College and, later, Georgia Southern University. She wants to pursue a doctoral degree in sociology and psychology. She says, "The things that have happened in my life have made me stronger and have helped me to depend more upon myself."

GEORGIA

Kathleen Spivak
John McEachern High School, Powder Springs, Georgia

"I can accomplish anything I set my mind to," says Kathleen. A member of National Honor Society and Beta Club, Kathleen is working hard to make her dream of a college education come true. She was once named All American Scholar by the U.S. Achievement Academy, and has won an accounting award. Kathleen has spent a lot of time with DFACS, a social program for disadvantaged youth. She is planning to earn a master's degree in psychology at Kennesaw State

College. "I want to help children cope with their problems," she says. "I want to help children turn their negative experiences around to their advantage."

HAWAII

Krystal Kim
Wallace R. Farrington High School, Honolulu, Hawaii

"When people set their hearts, minds, and souls into doing something, they find that they can work wonders, especially when they work together," says Krystal. Ranked at the top of her class, Krystal has served as president of National Honor Society, and was named Hawaii's National Scholar. She is active in leadership and has served throughout high school on student council and class council. She is also active in marching band and wind symphony. She plays basketball and has been on the cross-country team. Krystal

enjoys serving as an usher at the University of Hawaii's theatre productions. She hopes to attend Stanford University where she will major in English and minor in business. Krystal is planning a career in business.

HAWAII

Leilani Matayoshi
James B. Castle High School, Kaneohe, Hawaii

In the top five percent of her class, Leilani is a member of National Honor Society. She has participated in the Navy Honors program sponsored by the U.S. Navy. She has also participated in the Physics Olympics. An avid leader, Leilani has served as a senator to the Senate Protocol, and was a representative of Nazarene Youth Leader, as well as the Castle Complex Leadership Camp. She is also a member of the cross-country team. She hopes to attend Pacific University in Oregon, but is undecided about her major. "I want to

pursue a career in the medical area such as physical therapy, optometry, or pharmacy," she says. She is self-motivated and says, "Something inside me wants to excel."

IDAHO

December Ariwite
Blackfoot High School, Fort Hall, Idaho

A leader in her school, December was once president of student government. She has served in a leadership role in Key Club throughout her high school career. In addition, she has served as an officer in Business Professionals of America, Indian Club, and AISES. She is a member of National Honor Society and Natural Helpers. December's awards include Outstanding Business Student and Torch. She also served as her school's representative to the Hugh O'Brian Youth Leadership seminar. She says her club experiences have taught her "to give back to the com-

munity." She plans to attend Harvard or the University of Minnesota. She will major in business administration and minor in international business. December says, "I have striven hard to attain my goals."

IDAHO

Tracy Follett
Bonneville High School, Idaho Falls, Idaho

A solid student, Tracy is a sports enthusiast. She has played for both the tennis and volleyball teams. She has also participated in Key Club, Natural Helpers, and choir. Tracy has done volunteer work in hospitals and for the elderly. Her plans include going to Brigham Young University in Utah and majoring in nursing. A people person, Tracy says, "I want a career in a hospital so that I can work with different kinds of people." Tracy has numerous family responsibilities and she says she is serving as a role model to her younger siblings. "I want them to be the best they can possibly be," she says.

ILLINOIS

Esther Bit-Ivan
Mather High School, Chicago, Illinois

Ranked number one in her large class, Esther has served as president of National Honor Society. She has also served as vice president of Key Club and as a freelance writer for the school paper. Esther plays on the volleyball and basketball teams. She also participates in concert orchestra, Assyrian Club, and Russian Club. She has received Kodak's Young Leader Award and the Xerox Award. Her goal is to attend DePaul University in Chicago and major in pre-medicine. She says, "It is important for me to do well because I am setting an example for my younger brothers. I enjoy the challenge."

LLINOIS

Nina Dekelaita
Mather High School, Chicago, Illinois

In the top five percent of her class, Nina is a member of National Honor Society and the Advanced Placement Club. She has served as president of Key Club and as academic advisor on the yearbook. She also participates in Assyrian Club and her church choir and youth group. Her volunteer work includes tutoring. She plans to attend Loyola University in Chicago where she will major in early childhood education. Nina places a high value on education. She wants to be a teacher where she can "encourage my students to work hard and accomplish their goals."

INDIANA

Demetrius Sutton
Harrison High School, Evansville, Indiana

A member of the National Honor Society, Demetrius recently won the 21st Century Scholar Award. In school, she is active in peer mediation, Braves Against Drugs, and concert choir. She has had lead roles in school musicals. Demetrius is also active in her church, serving as vice president of the youth board. She has volunteered for a nursing home and Habitat for Humanity. Demetrius maintains a part-time job throughout the year. She plans to attend Indiana University, where she will major in medicine. Her dream is to work in pediatrics or child psychology. She says, "My future is important to me. I have set goals for myself, and I hope to one day attain them."

IOWA

Melanie Hall
Glidden-Ralston Community School District, Glidden, Iowa

Music is very important to Melanie, who is a member of her school's jazz and concert band, as well as the show and concert choir. An Iowa All-State Musician, Melanie wants to teach music or drama. She has participated in drama throughout her high school years, and has received the All-State Drama Award. Melanie has also lettered in basketball. Ranked at the top of her class, she is a member of National Honor Society. Her other interests include Spanish Club, student council, Science Club, photography, and the school newspaper. She has done extensive volunteer work, including performing for nursing home residents. Melanie plans to attend Northwestern University, where she will major in musical performance and education. She says, "I want to help students reach their full potential and develop their talents."

JAMAICA

Michelia Gooden
Morrison Technical High School, Montego Bay, Jamaica

Michelia's motto is, "Only hard work will lead to success, and I am aiming for success." Ranked at the top of her class, Michelia has received an award in English. She has participated in Key Club, History Club, and Environmental Watch Club. She has also done volunteer work with her church youth group. Michelia has worked part time throughout her high school years. She plans to attend Montego Bay Community College. Eventually, she hopes to earn a degree in business. Michelia says, "I want to become one of Jamaica's most successful businesswomen."

KANSAS

Christi Adcox
McLouth High School, McLouth, Kansas

A solid student, Christi has participated in Students Against Driving Drunk, the National Nutritional Council, and basketball. Her volunteer work has included tutoring and baby-sitting. She works part time throughout the school year, and hopes to attend Kansas State University at Manhattan. She will major in elementary education, and wants to be a teacher in a small town. Christi says of herself, "I am a strong-willed person who takes nothing for granted."

KANSAS

Kimberly Fuchs
Shawnee Mission N. High School, Merriam, Kansas

In the top 10 percent of her class, Kimberly is a member of National Honor Society and a recent recipient of the Xerox Award. Always involved in student council, she is president this year and has also served as secretary. She has been a cheerleader since ninth grade, and serves as captain this year. Kimberly is also involved in drama and is a member of Advanced Repertory Theatre and Thespian Troupe. She also participates in Spanish Club and every summer she works full time as a lifeguard. Kimberly plans to attend Harvard. Eventually she wants to be a psychologist. In a poem she has written called "Strength," Kimberly says, "You have control, believe it or not! Reach for your dreams when they're all that you've got!"

KENTUCKY

Maryfrances Cooper

Rowan County Sr. High School, Morehead, Kentucky

Maryfrances enjoys being a part of her school's speech team, and was recently a quarter-finalist in a speech tournament. She is a member of National Forensics League and Thespians. She also participates in Fellowship of Christian Athletes, soccer, Science Club, and Anchor Club. She has been a Girl Scout throughout high school. She volunteers as a teachers' assistant, and also babysits. Maryfrances hopes to attend Oral Roberts University in Oklahoma. She will major in chemistry and minor in biology. Her dream is to become a chemist in a laboratory. "I want to discover the cure for many diseases," she says.

KENTUCKY

Mona Eads

Madison Southern High School, Berea, Kentucky

Ranked in the top 10 percent of her class, Mona is a long-time member of Beta Club. She also participates in student council, show choir, Drama Club, and Fellowship of Christian Athletes. She is especially involved with dance team and has received many awards from that group, including Junior of the Year, Leadership, and Hardest Worker. Her volunteer work includes being a sign language interpreter at her church. She works part time throughout the year. Mona hopes to attend Eastern Kentucky University in Richmond, where she will major in deaf education. Her goal is to teach at a school for the deaf.

LOUISIANA

Ashley Barton

Grant High School, Dry Prong, Louisiana

Ashley has served as an officer in every group she has joined. She has served as president of student council, 4-H Club, Drama Club, and Fellowship of Christian Students. She has served as secretary of Students Against Driving Drunk, and was captain of her summer softball league. She has also participated in the Student Advisory Board, All-State Youth Choir, Young Ministers Institute, and the District Literary Rally. She has won a state award in 4-H, and has attended state conventions for student council and SADD. Her volunteer work has included serving as a church camp counselor. She works full time in the summer. Ashley wants to attend Northwestern State College in Natchitoches, but she is undecided about her major. "I want a career in which I will work with people," she says.

LOUISIANA

Katie Daigle

Thibodaux High School, Thibodaux, Louisiana

In the top 10 percent of her class, Katie is on the honor roll and has received awards as Top Scholar. She is a member of her school's band and marching band. Recently, she attended the Future Business Leaders of America Leadership Conference. Katie works at a part-time job throughout the year. She hopes to attend Nicholls State University in Thibodaux. She will major in business management and minor in auditing. Her dream is to own her own accounting business one day.

MAINE

Shannon Hussey
Biddeford High School, Biddeford, Maine

A determined student, Shannon spends much of her time tutoring and caring for children. She hopes to attend the University of Maine at Farmington. She will major in education and minor in social services. Her goal is to be a teacher at the primary level. She says, "I have courage and patience to reach my goals."

MAINE

Dovid Muyderman
Portland High School, Portland, Maine

An able student, Dovid has participated in the Academic Decathlon. He enjoys speech and debate and has served as co-president of the school's team. Recently, he won the Outstanding Speaker award in a regional debate. He also participates in Drama Club, Yes Diversity, chorus, and yearbook. He has volunteered with Boys and Girls Club, and has served as a peer helper at the teen center. He hopes to attend New York University. He will major in dramatic arts and minor in music. "I want to produce a movie about my life," he says. He is considering a career in psychology or law.

MARYLAND

Leema Basharyar
Seneca Valley High School, Germantown, Maryland

While taking a difficult course load, Leema has become a visible leader in her school. She has served as class president and president of National Honor Society. She has also chaired Students Against Driving Drunk, and was historian of French Club. Other activities include Spanish Club, soccer, and volleyball. Leema has also participated in Minds in Motion and a science contest called Final Frontiers. She has a part-time job throughout the year. Leema hopes to attend Georgetown University, and will major in chemical engineering and minor in architecture. She says, "College will be an exciting, challenging experience for me. But with hard work, commitment, and dedication, I will accomplish my goals in college and beyond."

MARYLAND

Kristi Masimore
North Carroll High School, Hampstead, Maryland

In the top 10 percent of her class, Kristi is a member of National Honor Society. Her other interests include yearbook, international studies, student government, Girl Scouts, Drama Club, and softball. Recently, Kristi attended Girls State and the National Youth Forum. Her activities have given her the opportunity to volunteer for several projects sponsored by her church, Girl Scouts, and National Honor Society. Kristi also has a special interest in working for the Huntington's Disease Foundation. In addition to her volunteer work, Kristi has a part-time job throughout the year. She plans to attend Johns Hopkins University, where she will major in pre-medicine. She has always dreamed of a medical career, and is especially interested in pediatric cardiology.

MASSACHUSETTS
Kyla Perfetuo
Randolph High School, Randolph, Massachusetts

Ranked near the top of her class, Kyla is a member of National Honor Society. She is also active in student government, and has served as class treasurer. Other activities include cheerleading and peer leaders. She has also received awards in biology. In addition to volunteering for worthwhile projects through her student activities, Kyla works part time throughout the year. She is planning to attend Brown University in Rhode Island, where she will major in marketing and minor in psychology. She says she wants to earn a master's degree, then work to the top in the field of marketing. Kyla has written many sayings that help her reach her goals. One of her favorites is, "Accept the things I cannot change; change the things I can."

MASSACHUSETTS
Yiomara Santiago
Marlborough High School, Marlborough, Massachusetts

A strong student, Yiomara has enjoyed field hockey and working on the school yearbook. She spends much of her time volunteering at a local hospital, and has received an award for her work. In addition, Yiomara works part time throughout the year. She plans to attend Saint Joseph's College in Maine, or the University of Massachusetts at Amherst. She will major in pre-medicine and minor in psychology. Her dream is to become a cardiologist. She says, "School is very important to me. The responsibility of putting myself through college will give me self-satisfaction."

MICHIGAN
Annamaria Barile
Lee M. Thurston High School, Redford, Michigan

Actively involved in her school's theatre arts program, Annamaria is in the varsity choir and concert choir. She has performed in a number of musicals and has received awards for her singing ability. She also participates in the Drama Club, and has been recognized for her performances. Annamaria greets her classmates each day over the PA system with her morning program, which she writes and hosts. She is a member of student government, student council, and Science Club. Annamaria works part time throughout the school year. She plans to attend Wayne State University in Detroit, where she will major in elementary education and minor in musical theatre performance. "I want to work with children," she says. "You can do what you want to do when you believe in yourself."

MICHIGAN
Nicholas Yu
Lee M. Thurston High School, Redford, Michigan

An able student, Nicholas has shown promise as a performer. He recently starred in his school's production of "Hello Dolly." He is a member of concert choir, and also the elite chamber singers. He plans to attend the University of Michigan at Ann Arbor. He will major in pre-medicine and minor in music theatre. He says he has always wanted to be an actor. "I will train as an anesthesiologist so that if I never become a performer I will have something to fall back on."

MINNESOTA

Nichole Shelquist
Bagley High School, Bagley, Minnesota

Ranked in the top 10 percent of her class, Nichole is consistently on the school honor roll. She is active with Drama Club and the yearbook staff. She enjoys tutoring at the local elementary school, and also volunteers at a day care center. In addition, she works nearly full-time throughout the year. Nichole wants to attend Minnesota State University at St. Paul, where she will major in psychology. She says, "I've thought about many different careers, and I know I want to do something that will help people who need and want help."

MINNESOTA

Brian Zirbes
Melrose High School, Melrose, Minnesota

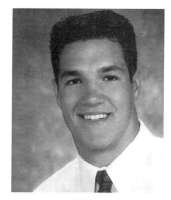

A member of the National Honor Society, Brian is ranked in the top 10 percent of his class. He enjoys sports and has served as captain of the varsity football team and as weight lifting supervisor. He has also served as vice president of student council. Recently, he represented his school at Boys State, and has served as a legislative page for the Minnesota House of Representatives. Brian spends a lot of time working on his parents' farm. His goal is to attend North Dakota State University at Fargo. He will major in athletic training. He says, "I would like to work on a college or professional sports team, then go back to school to earn a teaching certificate."

MISSISSIPPI

Natalie Burton
Pass Christian High School, Pass Christian, Mississippi

An honor roll student, Natalie has been a member of Students Against Driving Drunk, Interact, and Junior Co-op. She has served as an officer in each of these organizations. She has also received an academic achievement award from the English department at her school. She spends much of her time volunteering at local nursing homes and tutoring elementary students in English. She hopes to attend the University of Southern Mississippi, where she will major in psychology or business. She says, "I want a career that will allow me to learn and help make a difference in my life as well as others, whether it is through psychology or business."

MISSISSIPPI

Johnnie Collins
Cathedral High School, Natchez, Mississippi

A motivated individual who says that anyone can make a goal a reality, Johnnie is a solid student who dreams of being a design engineer for the aerospace industry. He has been active in 4-H, and has served as a land judge. He also received a first place award for seed identification. He has been a member of Students Against Driving Drunk, and has tutored students after school. He has also been a group leader in summer camp. He hopes to attend Georgia Tech. Johnnie says, "To face challenges in life, I use two main elements: persistence and optimism. I am motivated to achieve my goals."

MISSOURI

Nicole Kennedy
Oak Park High School, Gladstone, Missouri

A determined and dedicated student, Nicole helped to organize her school's first Future Business Leaders of America chapter. She has many family responsibilities and also works part time throughout the year. She hopes to attend the University of Missouri at Kansas City. She wants to major in child psychology. "I would like to work with children in some way," she says. If that career does not work out, she plans on becoming an accountant. "I like working with numbers," she says.

MISSOURI

Tenneille Patterson
Rolla High School, Rolla, Missouri

Ranked number one in her class, Tenneille is a member of National Honor Society, Octagon Club, Spanish Club, FCA, and student council. She also enjoys sports and is on the basketball, track, and cross-country teams. She participates in the school choir, and has received an award for a solo performance at the state level. As a volunteer, she has coached a girls basketball team, and has sung at community events. She works part time throughout the year. She plans to attend Washington University in St. Louis, where she will major in psychology. She says, "I want to continue my education, make my family proud, and create a sturdy foundation for myself."

MONTANA

Elizabeth Nadeau
Hamilton High School, Hamilton, Montana

A strong student, Elizabeth has received awards for speech and debate. She has also served on student council and is a member of the school choir. Active in Future Homemakers of America, Elizabeth has served as district president and state treasurer. In tenth grade, she was Miss Teen of Montana. She participates each year in the county fair, and has won awards for her crafts projects. Elizabeth works full time each summer at a day care center. She plans to attend Western Montana College in Dillon, and will major in elementary education. She says, "I would like to teach special education in an elementary school."

MONTANA

Mark Seitz
Darby High School, Darby, Montana

A long-time established leader at his school, Mark has served as student body president for the last two years. He is also district president of the Montana Association of Student Councils. His other leadership roles include Boys State, the Hugh O'Brien Youth Foundation, Montana Model United Nations, and the Montana YMCA Youth Legislature—where he served as House Speaker Pro Tem and assistant to the governor. He also participates in National Honor Society, band, Thespians, and Brain Bowl. He is ranked number one in his class. Each summer he works for a youth employment program. Mark plans to attend Carroll College in Helena, where he will major in political science and minor in theology. "Eventually," he says, "I would like to serve in government at the local, state, and federal levels. I want to be a public servant."

NEBRASKA

Celina Baldwin
Oakland-Craig High School, Oakland, Nebraska

A strong student, Celina is an active participant in Art Club, and has received awards for her art. She is also her class secretary. Celina has participated on the yearbook staff and on the track team. She works two jobs throughout the school year. Her dream is to attend Florida Southern University, where she will major in marine biology. In addition to wanting to find new species of aquamarine mammals, she says she may like to draw the skeletal system of mammals. "Challenges," she says, "make me strive harder to improve my standards."

NEBRASKA

Camekia Evans
Harry A. Burke High School, Omaha, Nebraska

Camekia has participated in African American Achievers and the University of Nebraska's Distinguished Scholars Program. She works part time throughout the year. Camekia hopes to attend the University of Nebraska at Omaha, where she plans to major in interior design and minor in business. Her dream is to own her own business one day. Camekia says, "I want to be somebody some day."

NEVADA

Michael Foster
Cimarron-Memorial High School, Las Vegas, Nevada

A sports enthusiast, Michael has been on the football team each year in high school. This year he played on varsity. He has also played basketball and track. During the summer, Michael worked full time as a camp instructor. He wants to attend Morehouse College in Georgia, or Mississippi State University. His goal is to earn a master's in elementary education. He says, "I am where I am today thanks to faith and family."

NEVADA

Lindsay Marshall
Earl Wooster High School, Reno, Nevada

Ranked in the top 20 percent of her class, Lindsay has received numerous awards in speech and debate. A long-time member of student government, she has served as a student body and class officer. She participates in the Vocational Industrial Clubs of America. Currently, Lindsay works at two part-time jobs. Her immediate goal is to attend the University of Nevada at Reno, where she will major in psychology and minor in criminal justice. Eventually, she hopes to work for the FBI. She says, "I have developed my inner strength and have become a positive person. I have grown from my experiences and will continue to do so in the future."

NEW HAMPSHIRE

Ben Woodward

Newfound Regional High School, Bristol, New Hampshire

Always listed on the honor roll, Ben is ranked in the top 10 percent of his class. He is active in sports, playing baseball and basketball for his school as well as a Babe Ruth traveling team. He is also active with class activities and E Cubed, a science group. Ben has played in advanced band and jazz band. He volunteers for charitable activities, and has tutored elementary students in Spanish. He works full time in the summer and part time during the school year. Ben hopes to attend Tufts University, where he will major in psychology and minor in business administration. He says, "I want to become a psychiatrist because I want to help others."

NEW JERSEY

Vanessa Flanagan

Kingsway Regional High School, Swedesboro, New Jersey

A hard-working, dedicated student, Vanessa is ranked in the top 10 percent of her class. Throughout her high school years, she has enjoyed participating in the Foreign Language Club. She spends most of her extra time, however, managing family responsibilities. Her dream is to attend Elon College in North Carolina or Rowan College in New Jersey. She wants to major in elementary education with an emphasis on special education. She is especially interested in teaching deaf children. She says, "I have the strength to face any challenge because I know I am worth the effort."

NEW JERSEY

Amit Malkani

N. Brunswick Township High School, N. Brunswick, New Jersey

Community service is something that Amit feels he must do. He volunteers many hours at several temples, a senior citizens center, a soup kitchen, and two local medical centers. "The joy I get from volunteering," he says, "cannot be bought. Through volunteering I have met many beautiful people who I have helped and who have helped me." In school, Amit is a solid student, ranked in the top 20 percent of his class and is a member of National Honor Society. He is treasurer of Future Business Leaders of America and co-chair of German Club. He is also a member of Key Club, Mathletes, and varsity tennis. He is planning to attend Siena College in New York, where he will major in medicine—a lifelong dream.

NEW MEXICO

Sarah Jimenez

Rio Grande High School, Albuquerque, New Mexico

A strong student, Sarah was recently elected to the Senate, which is her school's student government. She is president of Young Women's Organization, and has participated on the Prom Committee and yearbook. She is an excellent art student and has won several awards for her work, which has been displayed at the local shopping mall. She works full time throughout the school year. She plans to attend Utah Valley State College in Provo, where she will major in education art. Her goal is to teach art, interior design, and flower arranging. She says, "I want to help other deaf people and show them they can accomplish their goals."

NEW YORK

Kimberly Mullen
Martin Van Buren High School, Queens Village, New York

Ranked near the top of her class, Kimberly is on the Principal's Honor List, as well as Foreign Language Honor Society and Arista Honor Society. She works part time throughout the school year. She would like to attend New York University or Fordham University. She will study information systems and finance. She says, "I hope to become either a stockbroker or a systems analyst in a large corporation in Manhattan. Through college, I will be able to obtain the tools I need to reach all my goals and overcome all my obstacles."

NEW YORK

Natacha Zamor
A. Philip Randolph High School, New York, New York

Natacha, an able debater, led her debate team to five victories in the citywide Lincoln-Douglas debates. She has served as captain of the team for the last two years. Natacha is also involved with the Student Borough Council Committee and Chancellors Student Council Committee. She is a peer leader and a member of Computer Club. On Saturdays, Natacha participates in a neurobiology class given at Columbia University. She also represents her school in 3rd Millennium 30. She is a member of her church choir, the Usher Board, and the Women's Missionary Board. She also works full time during school vacations. Natacha hopes to attend Brown University in Rhode Island. She will major in law, with a concentration on immigration law. She says, "I would like to educate immigrants about their rights, duties, and responsibilities as members of American society."

NORTH CAROLINA

Jennifer Allebach
Seventy-First High School, Fayetteville, North Carolina

Ranked first in her large class, Jennifer is a member of National Honor Society. She also participates in debate and has won several speech awards from the National Forensics League. Other interests include yearbook, German Club, Pep Club, and Girl Scouts. She is an active volunteer with her church youth group. Jennifer plans to attend Harvard. She will major in government and economics, and minor in international relations. Later, she hopes to attend law school. Jennifer says, "I have a true wanderlust in me for new places, people, and experiences." Her dream is to one day run for Congress and "really make a difference in the world."

NORTH CAROLINA

Yakhia Hill
East Forsyth High School, Kernersville, North Carolina

Yakhia has served as president and secretary of her church choir. At school, she has participated in the gospel choir and honors chorus, and has advised a children's choir. She is also active in National Honor Society, Anchor Club, Junior Deans, and French Club. Yakhia does volunteer work with her church youth missionary group. She works part time throughout the year. Yakhia plans to attend Hampton University in Virginia, or Howard University in Washington, D.C. She will major in pre-medicine. Her dream is to have her own medical practice one day. Yakhia says, "I will continue with my education until I complete all of my goals in life."

NORTH DAKOTA
David Brecht
Golden Valley High School, Golden Valley, North Dakota

Ranked first in his class, David has been on the honor roll every year of high school. He is also active in student council, and has served as secretary. When he was a sophomore, he attended a National Leadership Camp. He plays basketball, and has earned a varsity letter. David works part time during the school year and full time in the summer. He plans to attend North Dakota State University at Fargo and earn a degree in electronic engineering. He says, "I keep myself busy with work and school activities."

NORTH DAKOTA
Amber Engquist
Oakes High School, Oakes, North Dakota

A sports enthusiast, Amber has participated in basketball, volleyball, and track. Her volunteer work includes teaching at a volleyball camp and teaching a Bible class. She works part time throughout the year. Her goal is to attend North Dakota State University at Fargo and major in business. She describes herself as self-reliant and actively involved in school.

OHIO
Gina Lowe
EHOVE Career Center, Milan, Ohio

A good student, Gina has been involved with the Vocational Industrial Clubs of America, Students Against Driving Drunk, Leadership Core, Drama Club, and peer mediation. She has volunteered for community projects through her church and school activities. Gina works two part-time jobs throughout the year. She hopes to attend Ohio State University at Columbus. One of her jobs is in an orthodontist's office and that exposure has led her to dream of becoming an orthodontist herself. She says, "I have the conviction to succeed, and I know that I will make my dream come true."

OHIO
Bethany Zickefoose
Logan High School, Logan, Ohio

"I foresee many adventures in my future," says Bethany. Ranked near the top of her class, Bethany is a member of National Honor Society. She has served as a special columnist for the school newspaper, and has received several writing awards. She also participates in the Creative Writing Club. She is undecided about where she will go to college, but she plans to major in physics and astrophysics. She is especially interested in theory, computation, and original research. Bethany says, "I have goals and care about my work, my beliefs, and making something of myself."

OKLAHOMA

Brian Nelson
Westmoore High School, Oklahoma City, Oklahoma

Ranked at the top of his large class, Brian is vice president of National Honor Society. He also serves as vice president of Key Club. Other memberships include Spanish Club, Mock Trial, and Scholastic Team. He has received awards for the science fair and for his creative writing. He is an active volunteer with the Red Cross, along with other projects sponsored by the service groups to which he belongs. During the summer, Brian works part time. He plans to attend Washington University in St. Louis, Missouri, where he will major in pre-medicine. His goal is to become a pediatrician. He says, "I want to help treat and cure pediatric diseases."

OKLAHOMA

Mariea Smith
Valliant High School, Valliant, Oklahoma

A member of National Honor Society, Mariea is ranked near the top of her class. She is a cheerleader, and has served as squad captain twice. She also participates in band, Science Club, Future Farmers of America, and basketball. Mariea has twice served as an officer of her class. She has a talent for public speaking and has received five first-place awards for her speeches from Future Farmers of America. Her volunteer work has included serving as a peer tutor after school. She plans to attend Oklahoma State University at Stillwater and major in medical science. "Helping others makes me feel wonderful," she says.

OREGON

Bart Barrett
Cove High School, Cove, Oregon

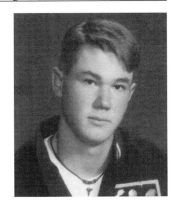

A good student, Bart is most enthusiastic about his sports. He has played football, basketball, and track through his high school years. He also enjoys participating in a community theatre group. For the last three years, Bart has spent his summers working on farms. His plan is to attend Western Oregon State University, where he will major in English and minor in drama. He wants to teach both subjects. "If my dream comes true," he says, "I will be the first member of my family to go to college."

OREGON

Nicole Hubbard
St. Mary's Academy, Portland, Oregon

A member of National Honor Society, Nicole is a strong student. She is president of German Club, and actively participates in Science Club, Graphic Arts Committee, and technical theatre. She has received awards in English, math, and science. Last summer, she worked full time for the Army Corps of Engineers. She hopes to attend Pomona College in Claremont, California. She will major in physics and minor in computer science. She will either be an electrical engineer, or return to her high school as a physics teacher. Nicole says, "Academic excellence is the way I will succeed."

OREGON

Katharine Jeans-Gail
St. Mary's Academy, Portland, Oregon

Katharine is a good student and a member of National Honor Society. She also participates in soccer, swimming, theatre and choir. Katharine is the president of Model United Nations. She has received awards as a scholar/athlete, and from Thespians. She has volunteered extensively, including time spent with the French American School as an assistant to a teacher. She works part time throughout the year. Katharine has not yet decided on a college, but says she will major in English and minor in biology. She wants a career where she can have a lot of interaction with the people in her community, and is interested in becoming an obstetrician.

OREGON

Damon Smythe
Jesuit High School, Lake Oswego, Oregon

Always on the academic honor roll, Damon is a recipient of the scholar/athlete award. He plays varsity football, basketball, and track and field. During the summer he has served as an athletic instructor and a camp counselor. He works part time throughout the year. Damon hopes to attend the University of California at Berkeley or the University of Colorado at Boulder. He will major in business and minor in English. He is interested in pursuing a career in international business, which may have been inspired when his family hosted a Japanese student a few years ago. Damon says, "I believe in myself and in my future."

OREGON

Morgan Thomas
Bandon High School, Bandon, Oregon

Ranked in the top 10 percent of his class, Morgan is a member of National Honor Society. He has served as vice president of his class, and he plays basketball. His volunteer work has included coaching a youth basketball team. He plans to attend the University of Oregon at Eugene, where he will major in biology and minor in psychology. He is also interested in journalism. Morgan says, "I am devoted to maintaining a happy and healthy life. I plan to achieve a good education and become a benefit to my community."

OREGON

Gregory Zimel
Jesuit High School, Portland, Oregon

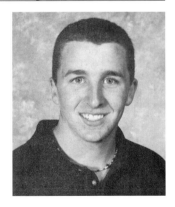

A good student, Gregory is on his school's honor roll. He has received awards in French and geometry. He has served as a camp counselor in addition to other volunteer activities. Gregory works part time throughout the year. He is undecided about where he will attend college, but he plans to study physical therapy. He says, "I want to set up my own clinic. I love to work with people and it would be great to see them recover. I have a basic love for humanity."

PENNSYLVANIA

Kevin Jones

Simon Gratz High School, Philadelphia, Pennsylvania

Ranked in the top 10 percent of his class, Kevin is a member of Philadelphia Future Scholars. He is a member of the Air Force Junior ROTC, and recently received an Outstanding Performance award. He is a peer mentor and has been a member of the school choir. Kevin is a poet and has received awards for his work from the Poetry Club. He is also active with the Drama Club. He works part time during the summer. Kevin plans to attend Morehouse College in Atlanta, Georgia. He will major in communications and English and minor in drama. Avidly

interested in all areas of entertainment, Kevin says he wants to be an actor, singer, writer, director, and producer. "There is nothing in the world that would be better for me than to go to college," he says.

PENNSYLVANIA

Erica Zermane

Wyoming Area High School, Exeter, Pennsylvania

A member of National Honor Society, Erica is an able student. She is active in Key Club, Drama Club, and softball. Recently, she was inducted into the International Thespian Society. In addition to volunteering many hours at a local hospital, Erica works part time throughout the summer. She plans to attend the University of Pittsburgh and major in physical therapy. She says, "I know I will be a caring, kind, sensitive hardworking physical therapist."

PUERTO RICO

Ida Gonzalez

Luis Munoz Rivera High School, Utuado, Puerto Rico

An excellent student, Ida is a member of her school's advanced placement group. She has received awards for her academic achievements throughout high school, including a first place award for the district science fair. Ida is active in AIDS prevention programs and fundraising efforts. She is also a counselor for students with drug problems. She has received a medal from the governor of Puerto Rico, as well as a plaque from the Municipal Assembly, for her volunteer work. She plans to attend the University of

Puerto Rico at Rio Piedras. She will major in communications. She says, "I want to keep on helping others and set a good example of leadership, persistency, and dedication."

PUERTO RICO

Osvaldo Martir

Patria Latorre, San Sebastian, Puerto Rico

A top student and member of National Honor Society, Osvaldo has received awards in math and science. He is active in Future Farmers of America, and has received high honors in contests involving vegetables. He is a member and former president of Environmental Club, and is also active in the Library Club. Each summer, he works part time for city hall. He also spends several hours each week tutoring children at the community center. Osvaldo plans to attend the University of Puerto Rico at Mayaguez

and major in industrial engineering. He says, "I plan to make life easier for the working people of our country by building or perfecting equipment used at their work place."

RHODE ISLAND

Mendy Miller

Scituate High School, North Scituate, Rhode Island

A member of National Honor Society, Mendy is ranked in the top 10 percent of her class. She has participated in the Rhode Island Scholar Athlete Games, and has been published by the National Library of Poetry. She is active with the International Order of Rainbow Girls and holds the position of worthy associate advisor. Also, she is the typing editor of the school yearbook. Mendy volunteers many hours each summer at a local hospital, and does peer tutoring during the school year. She plans to attend Northeastern University in Boston, where she will major in pre-medicine and minor in English. Her goal is to be a pediatrician in a children's hospital. She says, "I want to be a doctor to help save people from pain and suffering."

SOUTH CAROLINA

Richard King

Cheraw High School, Cheraw, South Carolina

On the honor roll each year of high school, Richard is ranked in the top 20 percent of his class. He plays varsity basketball, and is a former captain of the team. Richard works part time throughout the year. He wants to attend Coastal Carolina College in Conway, where he will major in mathematics and minor in business. He plans to go on and get a master's degree. Richard says, "With hard work, I will pursue and achieve my goals."

SOUTH CAROLINA

Danny Smith

Boiling Springs High School, Spartanburg, South Carolina

Danny says he faces his challenges one day at a time. A strong student, he has received awards for academic excellence and outstanding achievement. He plans to attend Spartanburg Technical College, where he will pursue a career in computers. Danny says, "I believe there is little I cannot do."

SOUTH DAKOTA

Alisha Hedman

T. F. Riggs High School, Pierre, South Dakota

Alisha, who enjoys playing volleyball, has volunteered at a local nursing home. She has had several full and part-time jobs. She hopes to attend Northern State University in Aberdeen, South Dakota, where she will major in pre-veterinarian medicine. Her goal is to become a veterinary technician, working on both large and small animals. Eventually, she would like to work at a zoo. Alisha says, "I am strong in my values and know what is important in life."

SOUTH DAKOTA

Benjamin Ready
Bennett County High School, Martin, South Dakota

Ranked first in his class, Benjamin is a member of the National Honor Society. He is president of the student council and has served as a class officer. He is also active in band, track, football, and basketball. Benjamin has attended the Hugh O'Brian Youth Foundation seminar, Boys State, and National Youth Leadership Conference. He is the recipient of the I Dare You award. Heavily involved with his church, Benjamin has served as youth leader and youth elder. He works at a part-time job through-out the year. Benjamin hopes to attend DePaul University in Chicago, where he will major in computer science. He says, "I am looking to the future and want to get a good education."

TENNESSEE

Mary Hall
Pickett County High School, Byrdstown, Tennessee

Ranked in the top 10 percent of her class, Mary is active in Spanish Club, Science Club, and band. She is the secretary and librarian for Band Council, and is an audio technician for the school choir. Mary also is a band reporter for a local TV station. In addition, she is the creator and publisher of band performance programs. She hopes to attend the University of Central Florida in Orlando. She will major in communications and minor in journalism. Mary describes herself as hard-working and talkative, which should serve her well in her career goal of becoming a TV news broadcaster.

TENNESSEE

Melissa Owen
Adamsville High School, Adamsville, Tennessee

A strong student, Melissa is active in 4-H, Senior Beta, and Future Homemakers of America. She works full time throughout the year. Melissa hopes to attend the University of Tennessee at Martin and major in pre-medicine. Her goal is to set up her own family practice clinic. She says, "I plan to come back and serve my community, to help the people who have helped and supported me."

TEXAS

Erin Evans
Robert E. Lee High School, Tyler, Texas

A member of National Honor Society, Erin is ranked in the top 20 percent of her class. She has received an award in history. A former school band member, Erin now is active with her church orchestra, youth choir, and Bible studies class. She plans to attend Hardin-Simmons University in Abilene, Texas. She will major in sociology and minor in early childhood education. Her goal is to counsel cancer patients. Erin says, "I have always worked hard toward academic success. Going to college will be a dream come true."

TEXAS

Misty Putnam
Arp High School, Arp, Texas

Ranked in the top 20 percent of her class, Misty is a member of National Honor Society. She is president of Art Club, and has participated in Future Farmers of America and Future Homemakers of America. She works part time throughout the year. Misty hopes to attend Kilgore Junior College, and wants to earn a degree in criminal justice. She says, "I would feel great if I knew someone changed for the better because of receiving a little help from me."

UTAH

Christian Nielson
Sky View High School, Smithfield, Utah

A hard-working, self-motivated student, Christian is active in debate and yearbook. His main interests, however, center on drama. He has been an actor and stage technician in a number of school plays and musicals. Christian has received a fine arts letter and is a member of International Thespian Society. He works part time throughout the school year. Hoping to attend Brigham Young University, Christian will major in business administration and minor in cinematography. He says of cinematography, "It is all-encompassing and covers interests that are not quite expressed." He adds, "I have worked long and hard at school to ensure a good future."

VERMONT

Joshua Dion
Twinfield Union High School, Plainfield, Vermont

A strong student and member of National Honor Society, Joshua enjoys playing basketball and baseball. He has served as a teacher assistant, and has volunteered at the local library. Joshua works part time throughout the year. He wants to attend St. Anselm College in New Hampshire, where he would major in computer science. After earning a master's degree, Joshua hopes to combine his computer education with his interest in endangered species. He says, "Self-confidence should be the number one goal in life. You've got to be yourself. If you're not, who will be?"

VERMONT

Tracy Godfrey
Montpelier High School, Montpelier, Vermont

Tracy is the school president of the Vermont Teen Leadership program. She also represents her school on the Youth Advisory Council. She has participated in Students Against Driving Drunk, peer mediation, Earth Club, hockey, and lacrosse. Tracy works full time each summer. She hopes to attend Plymouth State College in New Hampshire. She will major in early childhood education. She says, "Teachers have played an important role in my life. I would like to do the same for others."

VIRGINIA

Aisha Lloyd
Martinsville High School, Martinsville

A solid student, Aisha is an accomplished debater. She is on the school debate team and has participated in the National Forensics League. She is treasurer of her school gospel choir, and also participates in Upward Bound, the school newspaper, and Future Business Leaders of America. With her church, Aisha is a junior usher and serves as a tutor to elementary school students. She works part time throughout the year. Aisha hopes to attend Rutgers University in New Jersey. She will major in journalism and minor in political science. Her dream is  to be a news reporter for a large newspaper or major magazine. In the distant future, she is considering law school. Aisha says, "The star that shines most brightly to me is my college star."

VIRGINIA

Tonisha Terry   *William Clay Parrish Scholar*
John F. Kennedy High School, Richmond, Virginia

R anked at the top of her class, Tonisha is a member of National Honor Society and National Spanish Honor Society. She has also participated in Future Business Leaders of America. She works part time throughout the year for a local hospital. Tonisha plans to attend the University of Richmond. She will major in English, and go on to law school after earning her undergraduate degree. Tonisha says, "I am proud of my ability to meet the challenges that I have faced."

WASHINGTON

Le An Kloepper
Nooksack Valley High School, Everson, Washington

A n honor roll student, Le An is active in drama at her school. She has also participated in basketball and track. She hopes to attend the University of New Mexico at Albuquerque. She will major in physical therapy. She has worked at part-time jobs throughout high school. Le An says, "I have lived through obstacles in my life which I am proud to say I have overcome. I know I am lucky."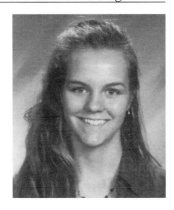

WASHINGTON

Michael Page
Connell High School, Connell, Washington

C onsistently on the honor roll, Michael has received numerous academic and citizenship awards. At school, Michael has participated in Natural Helpers, track, and basketball. He has also volunteered for a number of projects at his church. He works part time throughout the year. His plan is to attend Seattle Art Institute and major in computer graphics design. "I have been a fan of computer art and electronic games for a long time," he says. Eventually, he wants to produce his own projects and software design. Michael adds, "I look forward to continuing my education."

WEST VIRGINIA

Hanna Smith
Pocahontas County High School, Dunmore, West Virginia

Ranked near the top of her class, Hanna is a member of National Honor Society and is a National Merit Scholar. She has been a member of the Science Bowl team, math team, Artists' Guild, and Foreign Language Festival. She has also received awards in Spanish. Hanna hopes to attend Cornell University. She will major in astronomy and minor in art. After she earns her Ph.D., Hanna will apply to the astronaut guild. Hanna says she has become more of an individual over the last few years, and says she has excellent teachers to thank for helping her to love math.

WEST VIRGINIA

James Stitzel
Tygarts Valley High School, Mill Creek, West Virginia

A member of National Honor Society, James is ranked at the top of his class. He has participated in Quiz Bowl, and has served as president of Chess Club. Other activities include track, band, jazz band, band auxiliary, and Mind Games Club. James volunteers as a tutor and as a soccer coach. He also plays the piano for his church choir, and works part time each summer. James hopes to attend Cedarville College in Ohio. He will major in music education and minor in computer sciences. He

plans to one day earn a doctorate degree in music. James says he is thankful for his experiences in life, which have "forced me to grow and become the person I am today."

WISCONSIN

Christopher Hernandez
Waukesha North High School, Waukesha, Wisconsin

Active in school, Christopher enjoys wrestling, football, baseball, and Spanish Club. He is a member of National Spanish Honor Society, and has received his school's scholar/athlete award. Christopher works part time throughout the year. His plan is to attend Marquette University in Milwaukee, where he will major in biology and chemistry. He is considering a career as a physical therapist or a specialist in sports medicine. Christopher says, "I understand the value of a good education and work hard to achieve my goals."

WISCONSIN

Antonio McDaniel
Bay View High School, Milwaukee, Wisconsin

Ranked in the top 10 percent of his class, Antonio is a member of National Beta Club, National Honor Society, and Upward Bound. Active in sports, Antonio has served as captain of cross-country, basketball, and track and field. He has also served as president of Fighting Against Drugs with Education, and as vice president of Phi Sigma Gamma. Other interests include African American Club, peer mediation, and Boy Scouts Explorers. Antonio's awards include Athlete of the Year, and first place in the science

fair. Antonio wants to attend Marquette University and major in physical therapy. Later, he hopes to go to medical school and become a pediatrician. He says, "I set my own expectations."

WYOMING

Alicia Hansen
Kemmerer High School, Kemmerer, Wyoming

Ranked in the top five percent of her class, Alicia is a member of National Honor Society. She has also participated in drill team. Alicia works part time throughout the year. She hopes to attend the University of Texas of the Permian Basin in Odessa where she will major in psychology. Alicia says, "I enjoy talking to people and helping them solve their problems." She adds, "I have found that if you are willing to work hard and give things your best shot, you can accomplish anything you set your mind to."

WYOMING

James Kruse
Niobrara County High School, Lusk, Wyoming

A top scholar in his class, James is a member of National Honor Society. He has been active in 4-H, and has served as the club's treasurer, vice president, and historian. He also participates in Spanish Club, Teen Leadership Coalition, and drama. He works regularly on his family ranch. James plans to attend the University of Wyoming at Laramie. He will major in geology. He would like to work internationally so that he "can get paid to travel and experience other cultures." James adds, "I am working hard to fulfill my responsibilities."

KERRY HANSING

CAREER CENTER COORDINATOR
MT. DIABLO HIGH SCHOOL
CONCORD, CALIFORNIA

"I believe that all students can learn and have the right to try," says 1997 Horatio Alger Distinguished Educator Kerry Hansing. A career center coordinator at Mt. Diablo High School in Concord, California, Hansing encourages the students she counsels to work in a field they love and feel passionate about.

Hansing is a recent recipient of the Excellence in Education Award for Outstanding Career Center, given by the California Career Education Association. She has written grants for the school in the areas of self-sufficiency and gender equity. A college and career counselor for the last 12 years, Hansing says a professional educator has to truly like teenagers and recognize their intelligence and need for acceptance to be a successful counselor to them.

It is her job, says Hansing, to help students figure out what motivates them as well as what serves as a barrier to progress. "If I can remove the barriers, I can get students to be successful," she says. Hansing prides herself on making sure her students receive enough guidance so that they know not only what they want, but how to go about getting it. She says, "I gain their trust and confidence, and then help them pursue their goals. Our school has a high success rate of not only getting our students into college, but keeping them there long enough to earn their bachelor's degree."

In addition to her local responsibilities, Hansing serves on the Student Performance Committee for the Western Association of Schools and Colleges, is an advisor for the California Scholarship Federation, and is a supervisor for the SATs Educational Testing Service. She is also on the Advisory Committee for Diablo Valley College and the Gender Equity Council for the Mt. Diablo School District.

Horatio Alger Distinguished Educator Award recipients receive a $5,000 grant in the name of their schools to promote and enhance educational curricula and learning opportunities for students and faculty. Kerry Hansing plans to use the grant to develop a home-school communication program.

Getting parents involved is, according to Hansing, the key to keeping students successful in school. "Parents and schools need to team up," says Hansing, "but we need a method to communicate." Hansing believes that the school must reach out to parents, updating them on key issues related to college and careers. "Making parents come to the school to get information hasn't worked effectively for the majority of our parents," says Hansing.

The school's grant will be used to purchase equipment necessary to publish a monthly guidance newsletter for parents. In addition, Hansing is planning several teas to give parents the opportunity to come to school and meet with her. "In this way, we can give specific information for unique situations," she says. Hansing also hopes that these personal interviews will encourage more parent participation and volunteerism at the school.

Hansing explains that career planning is best accomplished when a student knows himself or herself first before deciding what to become. She enjoys quoting George Eliot, "It is never too late to be what you might have become." Hansing adds, "I feel education is lifelong and you must become your own teacher. It is my job to help students do that."

ANITA M. GLENN-RELLER

ADOLESCENT AND
FAMILY THERAPIST
RAINBOW FAMILY SERVICES

Anita M. Glenn-Reller, a 1990 Horatio Alger National Scholar from Shelton High School in Shelton, Washington, has been named the 1997 John W. Rollins, Sr., Alumnus of the Year. Selected from more than 200 eligible Horatio Alger National Scholars, Ms. Glenn-Reller will receive the Alumnus of the Year Award during the Association's 50th Annual Horatio Alger Awards Activities, April 24-26, 1997.

In addition to having faced difficult financial hardship as one of nine children, Ms. Glenn-Reller has also had to overcome traumatic abuse and a learning disability on her road to success. After high school, Ms. Glenn-Reller graduated from Pacific Lutheran University in Tacoma, Washington with a 3.0 grade point average. She went on to Barry University in Miami, Florida, where she received a master's degree in social work with a 3.5 grade point average.

Ms. Glenn-Reller, an adolescent and family therapist at Rainbow Family Services in McMinnville, Oregon, works with abused, neglected, and delinquent youth, and also is responsible for overseeing the agency's psychiatric/emergency shelter program. She has been a volunteer rape victim advocate and geriatric group therapist and a group therapist for emotionally handicapped individuals. Currently, she offers her time as a therapist for a group of high-risk boys at a local school and serves as a leadership skills group therapist.

Viewing herself as a role model for some of the troubled adolescents with whom she works, Ms. Glenn-Reller is proud she can serve as an example of someone who has conquered the odds and is involved in service to her community. "It gives me tremendous satisfaction to be able to instill in these youngsters a pride in their communities," says Ms. Glenn-Reller. "Many of them come from difficult backgrounds, and I am gratified to help them to reach higher and to help others."

Ms. Glenn-Reller currently is working toward her license in Oregon as a clinical social worker and plans to pursue a doctoral degree in therapy for children. As the 1997 Alumnus of the Year, she will receive an all-expense-paid trip to Washington, D.C., to attend the Awards Activities. In addition, a $5,000 contribution will be made in her honor to an approved 501(c)(3) charitable organization of her choice.

The Award, sponsored by John W. Rollins, Sr., recognizes outstanding National Scholars who have distinguished themselves by giving back to their communities and the nation, and who have become the next generation of America's leaders.

HORATIO ALGER ASSOCIATION OF DISTINGUISHED

Legacy

1957, 1967, 1977, 1987 Anniversary Classes

ADAM YOUNG

1957 Title
CHAIRMAN
ADAM YOUNG, INC.

Current Title
TREASURER & BOARD MEMBER
YOUNG BROADCASTING, INC.

> **"Opportunities will come your way. Recognize them and be ready for them."**

Working as a page for NBC when he was 16 years old, Adam Young began what he describes as "a wonderful life in the broadcast business." The oldest of eight children, Young left school and went to work in 1929, after his father lost his job during the Depression. He was just 15. After a year of menial jobs, he was offered the position as an NBC page.

The work was exciting and brought him into daily contact with the greatest show-business personalities of the day. Young watched while stars like Rudy Vallee, Fred Allen, and Jack Benny did their weekly radio shows from the NBC studio. When NBC moved to its present location at Rockefeller Center, Young became the first tour guide at NBC's huge new headquarters. After working in NBC's research department, Young attempted to break into the sales side of radio. NBC turned down his request for a transfer so he left and joined a small New York advertising agency.

Two years later, he joined a firm representing radio stations in the United States and Canada. He became sales manager, and developed an expertise for the Canadian radio market.

In 1944, Young opened his own firm with just two clients, but they were the two largest radio stations in Canada. Within two years, his company represented 50 Canadian stations. Soon, he was approached by U.S. stations and asked to represent them as well.

In 1984 he founded with his son Vincent Young Broadcasting, Inc., which owns 12 television stations. As YBTVA, it is on the NAS-DAQ exchange. The most recent purchase was KCAL Los Angeles, the great news and sports station owned by the Disney Company.

Of his Horatio Alger Award, Young says, "As a recipient I am pleased to have received it, but the more important thing is to get our message out to the youth of America. Young people need to understand what makes this country

work and operate. Anybody can make it if they work at it."

Though he finished only one year of high school, Young is a firm believer in education. During his working years, he got his general education degree at night and took many college courses. He also studied painting at the Museum of Modern Art in New York.

As someone who looks back on his life with satisfaction, Young defines success as "being in a position where you can direct your life." He also measures his success through the success of his children. He has two grown sons and a daughter whose personal and professional successes fill Young with pride. "Parents should remember to set a good example for their children. It's one of the most important things a parent can do. Give them something to follow. What you tell them may go in one ear and out the other, but the example you show them sticks."

> *"Don't run away from life.
> Never give up. Keep fighting
> and you will succeed. Above all,
> be a good leader."*

MAX COFFMAN

1967 Title
FOUNDER & CHAIRMAN (RET.)
MAMMOTH MART, INC.

Current Title
CONSULTANT
COFFMAN REALTY, INC.

When Max Coffman was honored as a 1967 Horatio Alger Award recipient, he was chairman of the board of a chain of 20 Mammoth Mart discount department stores that generated more than $50 million in sales annually. He sold his operations 10 years later, which then included 90 stores along the East Coast.

Coffman's success followed years of hard work and preparation. One of eight children born to immigrant parents in Quincy, Massachusetts, he started working at an early age, contributing to the family coffers by working as a delivery boy for local grocery stores.

After high school, he began his education in the retail field by working for a local department store, while attending Northeastern University at night. In 1935, he joined the predecessor company of Food Fair, and had the primary responsibility of opening new stores. Two years later, he was recruited by Stop & Shop, a leading New England food chain.

In 1946, Coffman ventured out on his own, operating a small chain of retail stores in New England. About 12 years later, he opened the first Mammoth Mart, in Framingham. Building the business was not without problems, but Coffman enjoyed the challenges. "It wasn't easy," he says, "but I never got discouraged—I just kept moving ahead. Too many people give up and run away from life at the first sign of trouble. But if you really want to do something with your life, you can solve the problems and make things work out. The future is only as good as you make it."

Throughout his career with Mammoth Mart and in the years after its sale, Coffman has been an active supporter of charitable, medical, and educational endeavors. He is a fellow at Brandeis University in Waltham, Massachusetts. He also serves as director of the National Jewish Hospital of Denver.

Coffman divides his time between his summer home in Brockton, Massachusetts, and his winter home in Hollywood, Florida. "We work hard, and we play hard too," he says. "We're having a wonderful time."

Coffman says his Horatio Alger Award reflects his personal philosophy. "If you work hard, opportunity will come along and you'll be ready for it," he says. To young people he offers this advice: "Be determined, work hard, run fast, fear nothing as you go up the ladder. Surround yourself with the best people you can find. Share responsibility, face reverses with determination, never give up. Keep fighting and you will succeed. Above all, be a good leader."

"Contribute to the betterment of humanity, in however small a way."

MICHAEL E. DEBAKEY, M.D.

1967 Title
CHAIRMAN OF SURGERY
BAYLOR COLLEGE OF MEDICINE

Current Title
CHANCELLOR EMERITUS
BAYLOR COLLEGE OF MEDICINE

As a child in a small Louisiana town, Michael DeBakey accompanied his parents each Sunday to a local orphanage, where they delivered clothes and food for the children. It was a lesson he never forgot. "Giving to others impressed me, and influenced my own determination to help others in any way I could."

Today, DeBakey is internationally recognized as an ingenious medical inventor and innovator, a gifted and dedicated teacher, a premier surgeon, and an international medical statesman. He was especially honored this year to serve as a consultant in Russia during Boris Yeltsin's heart bypass surgery.

When he received his Horatio Alger Award in 1967, DeBakey was chairman of surgery at Baylor College. Since then, he has been chancellor of Baylor College of Medicine from 1979 to 1996, president from 1969 to 1979, and chairman of the Department of Surgery and Olga Keith Wiess Professor of Surgery from 1948 to the present. He now serves as chancellor emeritus, distinguished service professor of surgery, director of the DeBakey Heart Center, and president of the DeBakey Medical Foundation.

Best known for his trailblazing efforts in treating cardiovascular diseases, DeBakey was a pioneer in developing an artificial heart, and was the first to use a mechanical heart pump successfully in a patient. Early in his career, working with Dr. Alton Ochsner, he linked smoking to lung cancer. While still a Tulane medical student, he devised a roller pump, which became an essential component of the heart-lung machine that launched open-heart surgery. He was also the first cardiovascular surgeon to do a successful coronary artery bypass, as well as the first successful carotid endarterectomy.

DeBakey was the son of a successful, self-made businessman who encouraged his son to strive for excellence. After his residency at Charity Hospital in New Orleans, he studied at the universities of Strasbourg and Heidelberg under two eminent medical scientists. He returned to the Tulane Medical School faculty until 1948, when he became chairman of the Department of Surgery at Baylor College of Medicine in Houston.

DeBakey founded and directed the Cardiovascular Research Center at the Texas Medical Center in Houston. In 1975, he established the first National Heart and Blood Vessel Research and Demonstration Center. In 1976, the Michael E. DeBakey International Surgical Society was founded; and two years later, the Baylor College of Medicine established the Michael E. DeBakey Center for Biomedical Research and Education. In 1985, the DeBakey Heart Center was established in Houston.

Author of more than 1,400 publications, he has written numerous books, including the *New York Times* best-seller, *The Living Heart*, and *The New Living Heart Diet*.

Recently, DeBakey said, "The road to success is paved with self-discipline, industry, and perseverance. My life and work have been guided largely by my parents instilling in me integrity, a reverence for life, and compassion for suffering humanity. I have done my utmost to help others preserve life and live it to the highest level of health, happiness, and personal fulfillment."

DeBakey has consulted with heads of state throughout the world. Among his innumerable prestigious awards are the Presidential Medal of Freedom, the highest American civilian award, the Presidential Medal of Science, and the Lasker Award for Medicine.

DeBakey says he is proud of his Horatio Alger Award and offers this advice to the Horatio Alger Scholars: "Always strive for excellence, and try to turn all adversities into successes."

Michael E. DeBakey, M.D.

> *"You make a living by what you get, but you make a life by what you give."*

When John Howard accepted the presidency of Rockford College in Rockford, Illinois in 1960, his biggest challenges were raising funds for a new 300-acre campus, reinvigorating the school's educational program, and widening its reputation for excellence in liberal arts. Seventeen years later, Howard completed an $18 million campaign, enabling the college to move to a new campus. Still, he was not satisfied. Increasingly, Howard was concerned about the changes in academic life brought on by the tumultuous 1960s.

In 1976 he established the Rockford College Institute. Convinced of the importance of its mission, Howard resigned as president of the college and became the institute's first director. Today, Howard is counselor to the Rockford Institute, which is one of this nation's leading think tanks and study centers. Now separated from Rockford College, the institute builds public understanding in four areas—religion, education, literature, and the family—areas Howard calls the four "value-forming systems" of a free society.

In March of this year, Howard's institute hosted the International Congress of Families in Prague. The group issued a declaration that the traditional family has to be the centerpiece of any workable society regardless of its form of government. Participants defined those social and economic circumstances that encourage the flourishing of family life.

In addition to those activities, Howard serves as president of the Ingersoll Foundation, the philanthropic division of the Ingersoll Milling Company in Rockford, Illinois. The Foundation awards two $20,000 prizes annually to authors whose works affirm the principles of Western civilization.

A thoughtful, deeply religious family man, Howard says his earliest inspiration came from his mother, who raised her three children single-handedly. "Life wasn't easy for her but she never complained." Howard left home to attend Princeton University, and contributed to the cost of his education with jobs in the summer and during the school year. He served in the Army in World War II, and earned a battlefield commission and two silver stars for bravery.

After the war, he went to Northwestern University, where he completed his B.S. degree and earned an M.A. in counseling and guidance. His first teaching job, at $50 a week, was at Palos Verdes College, in California. After four years, he became president; in 1956, he accepted an appointment as executive vice chairman of President Eisenhower's Committee on Government Contracts. After a year, he returned to Northwestern for doctoral studies in French literature. He then accepted the presidency of Rockford College, a position he held for 17 years.

Concerned about education today, Howard often writes opinion pieces for newspapers. "The central purpose of education," which Howard feels has been forgotten, "is to train each new generation in the ideals of their own society. For a society to sustain itself, character education or moral maturity is the absolute minimum essential of an educational program."

Honored to have received the Horatio Alger Award, Howard advises today's young people to "study the biographies of the great men and women of the past to learn integrity, truthfulness, humility, and piety as the features of a good life."

JOHN A. HOWARD, PH.D.

1967 Title
FORMER PRESIDENT
ROCKFORD COLLEGE
FOUNDER & RETIRED PRESIDENT
THE ROCKFORD INSTITUTE

Current Title
COUNSELOR
THE ROCKFORD INSTITUTE
PRESIDENT
INGERSOLL FOUNDATION

ELMER L. WINTER

CO-FOUNDER &
PRESIDENT (RET.)
MANPOWER, INC.

> **"You need the right idea . . . then you just work hard to make it happen."**

When Elmer Winter and his brother-in-law, Aaron Scheinfeld, two Milwaukee attorneys, opened the nation's first temporary employment service as a sideline to their law practice in 1948, they never dreamed that they were launching not just a new company, but a major new international industry.

Winter reports they lost $9,000 in their first year—a lot of money in those days. They thought of closing down the business, but they had a number of repeat customers, so they decided to go one more year. At the end of the second year, Manpower recovered its initial losses and made a small profit. The rest is history. Today, the company has more than 2,400 offices in 41 countries.

The thought that so many lives have improved because of Manpower's role is a constant source of pride to Winter. "We were one of the first service businesses to franchise," says Winter. "Many people come to see me today whose parents started a Manpower franchise in the fifties. Now they have joined their parents and are operating a successful family business. I get a kick out of seeing how happy and enthusiastic they are about it."

Winter received the Horatio Alger Award in 1967, and 10 years later the board of directors sold Manpower to the Parker Pen Company. Winter retired, but he continues to work full time each day in an office at Manpower in areas that interest him. One project is the Committee for Economic Growth for Israel. As chairman, Winter travels frequently to Israel, and often works as a "matchmaker" between U.S. and Israeli companies.

An avid interest discovered early in his retirement is painting. Winter continues to paint and recently won an award from a local public television station. "All through my life, what I have enjoyed most is being creative," he says. "I like to develop new ideas. I like new challenges. I get a great sense of satisfaction out of finding new ways to do things. When someone says it won't work, I say, 'Why not?' That forces them to think creatively, to think of ways to make it work."

Winter says he enjoys getting involved at the local level. He is convinced that to compete in today's world, students must be proficient in math, science, reasoning, and computers. At his high school alma mater, he set up a foundation whose goal is to make each graduate computer literate. Also, he works with elementary students to improve their math and science skills.

Winter, who is eager to show his Horatio Alger Award to office visitors, says he is encouraged to see how much the Horatio Alger scholarship program has grown over the years. "We have to train our young people for the jobs of the future," he says.

A good family life is what Winter believes you need to be happy. His wife of more than 50 years died six years ago. Today, Winter is remarried and enjoys his new wife, Hope, his three daughters, eight grandchildren, and one great-grandchild. "It's fundamental to wake up each morning to a happy family."

His recipe for success? "You need the right idea—something different, with a little flair," he says. "And then you just work hard to make it happen."

JOHNNY CASH

The life of an Arkansas sharecropper with seven children was difficult during the Depression, but family hymn singing around the piano made life tolerable for young Johnny Cash. In fact, music was a passion for Cash. He especially enjoyed listening to country singers on the radio. When his father told him he could no play the radio because they could not afford a new battery, 12-year-old Cash cried, "But I can't live without music."

Today, Cash's music has enriched the lives of millions during his 40-year career. He is the only entertainer in history to have been inducted into the Songwriters Hall of Fame, the Country Music Hall of Fame, and the Rock and Roll Hall of Fame. Known as a man of the people, Cash's music deals with universal emotions such as pain, heartbreak, despair, disappointment, and loneliness. Dozens of his hit records have become American standards, including such all-time favorites such as "Cry, Cry, Cry," "Folsom Prison Blues," "There You Go," "Big River," "A Boy Named Sue," and "I Walk the Line."

Born in a three-room railroad house in Kingsland, Arkansas, Cash was the fourth of seven children. His father, a cotton farmer, acquired a 20-acre plot of land from a federal land-grant program. Young Cash helped out by picking 350 pounds of cotton a day and hunting rabbits to put food on the table.

Cash taught himself to play the guitar when he joined the Air Force. Upon his release from the service, Cash married and studied radio announcing on the GI Bill. But when his wife got pregnant, he quit school and sold appliances door to door.

A friendship with two mechanics who were part-time musicians, Luther Perkins and Marshall Grant, launched Cash's career. The three formed a combo, Johnny Cash and the Tennessee Two. They auditioned with Sun Records, and "Hey, Porter," a song Cash wrote in Germany, was accepted for recording if Cash could write another good song for the flip side. He wrote "Cry, Cry, Cry." The record was released in 1955 and sold nearly 100,000 copies, reaching the best-seller charts within six weeks. For the remainder of the decade, Cash had each of his releases reach the Top 10 charts in the country-and-western music categories. He sold 6 million records and starred on *The Grand Ole Opry* radio show.

Appearances in films and as a star of his own weekly ABC TV program, *The Johnny Cash Show*, reestablished Cash as a major star in the 1970s. In his autobiography, *Man in Black*, Cash says he is "only completely alive" when he is performing and sharing with audiences the songs he loves.

Today, Cash continues the work he believes God has set out for him. "I never allow myself to be slothful or lazy. I have maintained my integrity through every struggle in life. I set goals for myself, and stay in communication with God and his will for me," says Cash, who has recently released a new album, *Unchained*. He won the Guitar Player of the Year award in 1995, and will be honored by the Kennedy Center in December for his life's work.

Looking back over his career, Cash offers this advice to today's young people: "Know your talents and potential. Never, never, never give up."

Of his Horatio Alger Award, Cash says, "It is an extremely prestigious award and I'm very proud of it. It makes me look again to my roots; to evaluate my opportunities against my efforts for success."

"If you put in a total effort, the rewards will come."

J. IRA HARRIS

1977 Title
SENIOR INVESTMENT BANKER
SALOMON BROTHERS, INC.

Current Title
SENIOR MANAGING DIRECTOR
LAZARD FRERES AND COMPANY

When Ira Harris played stickball with friends in his Bronx neighborhood, he knew the boys who could hit the ball the farthest were the ones to be reckoned with. Ira could hit it the length of three sewers. "Hitting a stickball three sewers was really important where I grew up," says Harris. "I still call that my proudest achievement."

The competitive nature that made Harris a leader in the streets of the Bronx catapulted him to national prominence in the fast-paced investment banking business. Armed with a degree from the University of Michigan, he began his financial career selling mutual funds door to door in New York. Soon he joined Granbery Marache, predecessor of Blair and Company, as a retail securities salesman. He began writing his own research reports, and soon developed a strong following among leading corporate executives.

In 1964, Blair sent him to Chicago to revive its faltering office there. The 26-year-old Harris soon turned the Chicago office into a leading money-maker. Within three years, he was hired by Salomon Brothers to build its investment banking presence in Chicago. He created an

aggressive outpost for them there, providing a full range of investment banking services. Through his expertise in corporate mergers and acquisitions, Harris brought major new clients to his firm. Recognized as one of the nation's most creative merger experts, Harris has closed some of the most important corporate deals in the past three decades.

One of the youngest recipients of the Horatio Alger Award, Harris was just 39 and a general partner at Salomon Brothers when he was so honored in 1977. In 1978, he was named a member of the executive committee at Salomon Brothers, and in 1981, when the firm merged with Phibro, he became an executive managing director and a member of the board of directors. In 1983, Harris resigned these management positions to devote himself full time to the investment banking business and continued with Salomon Brothers as a senior executive director. In 1988, he joined Lazard Freres & Company as a senior partner.

Harris is a director of Manpower Inc., Caremark International Inc., and Brinker International, Inc. He is a life trustee of

Northwestern University, a director of the Polk Brothers Charitable Foundation, a director of Northwestern Memorial Hospital, a member of the Kellogg Graduate School Advisory Board, a director of the Chicago Public Library Foundation, a life director of the National Center for Learning Disabilities in New York City, and a life trustee of the Museum of Science and Industry. He also serves as a director of the Big Shoulders Fund for the Chicago Parochial School System.

Hard work, ambition, and self-confidence all play a role in success, he says. "My parents pounded that work ethic into me—the belief that if you put a total effort into something, the rewards would come. I never really worried about failing. I just had a feeling I would do well in whatever I tried."

Still, Harris cautions that self-confidence must be tempered with patience. "It takes time to accomplish things. You have to be willing to put in the time to learn," he says. He adds, "The Horatio Alger Association recognizes people who are able to do that. Being named a member of the Association is one of my most cherished awards."

DAVID J. MAHONEY

1977 Title
PRESIDENT
DAVID MAHONEY VENTURES

Current Title
CHAIRMAN
THE CHARLES A. DANA
FOUNDATION

David Mahoney planned to return to the Wharton School of Business, where he had been a student before World War II interrupted his studies. To support himself until the fall term started, he got a job in the mailroom of a New York advertising agency. But after three months, the agency promoted him to assistant account executive. His new responsibilities, and the $50 a week, gave him second thoughts about going back to school.

His solution was typical of the versatility and drive that have been evident throughout Mahoney's fast-moving corporate career. He returned to school and kept the job, working days in New York and commuting each evening to Philadelphia for night school.

When he completed his degree less than three years later, he was a vice president at the agency and was supervising some of its key accounts. "In this world, things are constantly changing, and you have to be open-minded and flexible," says Mahoney. "If you can multiply flexibility with determination and knowledge, you've got it made."

Born in New York's East Bronx, Mahoney was the son of an Irish immigrant. His father, a crane operator, had a hard time finding construction jobs during the Depression. Young Mahoney sold newspapers at age nine to help out.

A scholarship of $10 a month enabled Mahoney to attend Cathedral High School, a private school in Manhattan. Later, he was awarded a scholarship to LaSalle Military Academy. A good baseball and basketball player, he next won an athletic scholarship to the prestigious Wharton School.

Two years after earning his degree, Mahoney left a comfortable $25,000-a-year ad agency job to form his own firm, established with a $10,000 bank loan. The young agency attracted some excellent clients, among them the Good Humor Corporation.

Five years later, Mahoney sold his agency for $500,000 and assumed the presidency of Good Humor. There, he increased sales and profits dramatically. In another five years, Mahoney joined Colgate-Palmolive as executive vice president of the firm's domestic operations. Four years later, in 1966, he was recruited by Norton Simon to head Canada Dry, which was controlled by Hunt Foods & Industries.

Within two years, Norton Simon, Inc., was created by a merger of Hunt Foods & Industries, the McCall Corporation, and Canada Dry. Mahoney was named president and chief operating officer, the number-three spot. A year later, he emerged as chief executive officer. When Simon retired at the end of 1969, Mahoney became president and chairman.

By 1977, when Mahoney was honored by the Horatio Alger Association, Norton Simon was a major international consumer products marketing company. In 1983, he left the firm to head his own investment company, David Mahoney Ventures, as well as the Churchill Trust Company.

Mahoney has had a life-long commitment to health and medical research. In 1983, he endowed the David Mahoney Institute of Neurological Sciences at the University of Pennsylvania. In 1990, he established the Harvard Mahoney Neuroscience Institute. Today, he is chairman and CEO of the Charles A. Dana Foundation, and the Dana Alliance for Brain Initiatives.

Mahoney says that success comes to those who are able to adapt to change. "You can't have pre-set ideas."

Of his Horatio Alger Award, Mahoney says, "It means a great deal to me. Our country is full of opportunities for those who work hard."

"Real joy comes from doing things for others."

RUTH STAFFORD PEALE

1977 Title
CHAIRMAN &
CHIEF EXECUTIVE OFFICER
FOUNDATION FOR
CHRISTIAN LIVING

Current Title
CO-FOUNDER
PEALE CENTER

The daughter of a Methodist minister in Detroit, Ruth Stafford longed to attend college. Since her family could not afford to finance a college education for her and her two brothers, she took a job with the Michigan Bell Telephone Company. Her earnings helped put her older brother, Charles, through Syracuse University. After he earned his degree, he helped pay Ruth's expenses at Syracuse. That early lesson in the joys and benefits of teamwork helped pave the way for a lifelong partnership with husband and co-founder of the Horatio Alger Association, Reverend Norman Vincent Peale.

In six decades of marriage and ministry, the Peale partnership communicated its message of the power of Christian faith and positive thinking to millions of people worldwide. More than 4 million people subscribe to the inspirational monthly magazine *Guideposts*, founded by the Peales in 1945. The nonprofit, interfaith publication carries no advertising. "It's a spiritual magazine that tells how people apply their religious faith to everyday life," says Peale, chairman of *Guideposts*.

The Peale partnership of Norman Vincent Peale and Ruth Stafford Peale has undergone many changes in the last decade.

Guideposts has increased to six the number of magazines it publishes, including *Angels on Earth* and *Miracles and Healing*. Both are fast-growing, successful publications.

A new building, the Center for Positive Thinking, was dedicated in Pawling, New York in 1988. Included in this large complex is a library, a display of memorabilia covering Norman's career, a Holy Land Museum, and samples of a POPS (Power of Positive Students) program introduced into schools in 49 states, as well as telephone lines to 800 numbers for prayer requests.

A 90th birthday party for Norman was held on May 31, 1988 at the Waldorf-Astoria Hotel in New York. Norman wrote his 46th book during this time.

Unfortunately, on December 24, 1993, Norman Vincent Peale, passed away, but Ruth has carried on with their work. At Norman's funeral service, she offered a free copy of Norman's bestselling book *The Power of Positive Thinking* to anyone who would write to her. She gave away more than 100,000 copies of the book that has been a bestseller since 1952.

Two 50th anniversaries were celebrated—Peale Center in 1990 and

Guideposts magazine in 1995.

In 1996, Peale Center and *Guideposts* magazine, both nonprofit organizations, merged to form Guideposts—A Church Corporation, with Peale Center serving as the Outreach Division. Peale Center operates the School for Practical Christianity for clergy and spouses, which meets in various parts of the country twice a year. The Center also offers a prayer ministry, which handles more than 10,000 prayer requests each month, and conducts a leadership conference for business executives.

Peale continues to enjoy her farm in Pawling, New York, going to her office at Peale Center daily, and traveling to speaking engagements. She has three children, eight grandchildren, and four great-grandchildren.

"My entire life has been devoted to helping people find a richer, fuller life for themselves and their family," says Peale. "It has been a privilege to write and speak about discovering that God is ever-present in our lives. He brings spiritual strength to all of us. The motivation I have received from Horatio Alger participants has been a blessing to me."

ANN PERSON

FOUNDER & PRESIDENT
STRETCH & SEW, INC.

Ann Person was only five when she stuck her finger with a sewing-machine needle for the first time. It was a prophetic beginning to a lifelong involvement with the art and craft of sewing.

Born in the backwoods of the Pacific Northwest, Person grew up in a small house built by her father which had no electricity or running water. Her mother, a seamstress, taught her to sew, and she studied industrial sewing in high school, then attended the University of Oregon as an art major.

She interrupted her studies to join the WAAC during World War II. As a Wac, she taught painting in an Army convalescent hospital. After the war, she married, and she and her husband embarked on a series of disappointing business ventures.

Following a serious automobile accident that left her disabled for two years, Person decided to concentrate on her primary interest, sewing. She began giving sewing lessons and experimenting with stretch-knit fabrics, which were just coming into popularity. She developed a special technique for sewing knits, and began designing special patterns, cutting them from brown butcher paper for her students.

The same year Person opened her first store, she wrote an instruction book about her technique. It became an overnight success. The book led to a syndicated television show, *Sewing with Ann Person*, and made a household name to millions of American women. Person remembers that time proudly. "The method of sewing I developed gave women a sense of achievement that was not possible with the old methods. Women felt they had done something beneficial for their own self-image."

In the decade from 1967, when the first Stretch & Sew Fabric Center opened in Burns, Oregon, to 1977, when Person won her Horatio Alger Award, Stretch & Sew grew to a chain of more than 200 franchise stores, doing $74 million a year in sales. In the early 1980s, however, knits fell into disfavor and Person's business experienced some difficult times. As president of Stretch & Sew, and in an effort to help the remaining stores, Person changed from a franchising company to a licensing company. This eliminated overhead for the franchisee, and allowed the company to market its products on the open market.

Today, Stretch & Sew is a thriving company with more than 2,000 accounts in the United States and Canada. Many customers who bought patterns and books and took classes in the many Stretch & Sew stores still love to sew and, in many cases, have passed that love on to their offspring. With the resurgence of knits into the fashion scene, Person is amazed at the wonderful growth the company is experiencing.

When asked about her success, Person says she had a burning desire to do something meaningful. "I was willing to do whatever had to be done to be successful," she says. "I had drive, energy, determination, desire, and a positive attitude."

Person's Horatio Alger Award came at a time when her career was at an all-time high. "It was wonderful to be recognized for my accomplishments at a time when few women were entrepreneurs. I'm proud of my award and the personal success it symbolizes."

Person believes in living life to the fullest. "You should," she says, "accomplish whatever it is you are capable of. Use your God-given talents, and give something to the world that can be passed on to future generations."

"Don't believe everything you see and hear; make your own judgments."

ROGER TORY PETERSON*

ARTIST, WRITER, NATURALIST

Roger Tory Peterson began his lifelong love affair with birds at age 11, when he joined a Junior Audubon club. Known internationally as the man who revolutionized bird-watching and nature study, this 1977 Horatio Alger Award winner has encouraged and enabled millions throughout the world to share his love for birds and other wildlife through his writing, painting, photography, and teaching.

Born in Jamestown, New York, Peterson was the son of a Swedish immigrant. Although the family was poor, young Peterson's love for birds was so great that he spent every spare penny he earned from odd jobs to buy bird seed and, eventually, a camera. His father, a cabinetmaker, disapproved of his son's obsession. But Peterson saw birds as great symbols of freedom and liberty. "Birds have wings; they're free; they can fly where they want when they want," he says. "They have the kind of mobility many people envy."

Peterson's skill in sketching birds got him a job in a furniture factory, painting Chinese designs on lacquer chests. After completing high school, he went to New York to study at the Art Students' League and the National Academy of Design.

While teaching science and art at the River School in Brookline, Massachusetts, Peterson continued to compile paintings of birds. He took his idea for a simple bird guide to five publishers before Houghton Mifflin agreed to publish 2,000 copies of *Field Guide to the Birds*. The first press run sold out in less than a week, and has been Houghton Mifflin's best-seller on any subject over the past 60 years. This book was followed by a series of other guidebooks to wildlife and natural history subjects ranging from butterflies and wildflowers to animal tracks and shells. Each volume of the Wildlife Guide series, now numbering 50, features the "Peterson System" of identification.

By serving as "an interpreter between the scientist and the layman," Peterson's work has increased public appreciation of nature and wildlife conservation. "Birds are indicators of the environment," he says. "If they are in trouble, we know we'll soon be in trouble."

Peterson's gallery paintings of birds have been exhibited in dozens of museums and have become collector's items. He is the recipient of 23 honorary degrees in science, letters, and fine arts, and has received numerous awards in recognition of his contributions to science, education, and conservation, including the Presidential Medal of Freedom in 1980.

An internationally known lecturer, filmmaker, and photographer, Peterson has been credited with helping to build the modern environmental movement. In recognition for the impact of his work, he has been twice nominated for the Nobel Peace Prize.

A book recently published by Rizzoli, *Roger Tory Peterson: The Art and Photography of the World's Foremost Birder*, gives a good chronology of his work, showing its development from earlier beginnings to its present form.

In 1993, the Roger Tory Peterson Institute of Natural History was dedicated in Jamestown, New York to carry on his work for future generations. The Institute's mission is to educate society about the natural world.

Peterson says of the future, "Not all is doom and gloom. We are beginning to understand the natural world and are gaining a reverence for life—all life."

*Roger Tory Peterson passed away in 1996. This was his last interview.

> *"Life is a great big book,*
> *and each day is a page.*
> *Once you turn the page,*
> *there is no turning back."*

ROSE COOK SMALL

1977 Title
VICE PRESIDENT &
DIRECTOR (RET.)
BLUEBIRD, INC.

Current Title
FOUNDER &
VICE PRESIDENT (RET.)
BLUEBIRD, INC.

The daughter of poor immigrants, Rose Cook Small was born and raised in Camden, New Jersey. To help her parents support their six children, Rose was selling produce on street corners by the age of 12. She dropped out of school before completing the 10th grade.

At 16, she married an ambitious young clerk in a local meat market, Harry Cook. While working in the shop with her husband, she dreamed of one day owning a large meat processing and packing business. That dream began to take shape in 1933, when Rose and Harry opened their own meat market. She was just 21, but she took on the major responsibility for the store in addition to raising their two small sons.

The market was so successful that the Cooks opened a second one in 1936, this time with a packing house. But a year later, the market was destroyed in a fire. Rose walked the 14 miles to the store to clean up the mess because she could not afford the eight-cent trolley fare.

Hoping to reopen the store, Rose went to her bank to get a loan. When the bank officers hedged, she offered her wedding and engagement rings as collateral. The loan was granted, and Bluebird, Inc. was established with the reopening of the second market in 1940.

The business flourished, and when her husband died a decade later, Rose decided to continue operating it. During the ensuing years, she learned every facet of the meat business, from buying to slaughtering to cutting meats.

By 1963, Bluebird had moved to a larger plant, and within five years was shipping 2 million pounds of meat weekly. She married Morris Small in 1960, and took the company public in 1968. Over the next decade, she acquired Agar Company, the Patrick Cudahy Company, and Mid-South Packers, thus building the largest and most proficient meat-processing plant in the United States.

When she received the Horatio Alger Award in 1977, Small's company was producing 14 million pounds of meat weekly and had annual sales of more than $400 million. Her son Herbert Cook was chairman of the board, while she remained active as a vice president and director.

Always involved in charitable and civic causes, Small always kept a box on her desk. Each morning, when she arrived at her office, she would put some money in the box. With each phone call that brought good news about her company, she would add more money. At the end of each week, for 20 years, she sent the contents of the box to the Little Sisters of the Poor.

She also raised funds for a summer camp for underprivileged children, for local synagogues, and for a Catholic church in Philadelphia. In memory of her husband, she contributed funds for a room at Children's Memorial Hospital at the University of Pennsylvania.

Of her Horatio Alger Award, Small says, "It was an honor to be selected for this prestigious award. Starting a business and making it work isn't easy, but with hard work and dedication I believe anything can be accomplished. My award is the physical symbol of how I made my dream come true."

127

1977 Award Recipient

L. HOMER SURBECK

WALL STREET ATTORNEY (RET.)

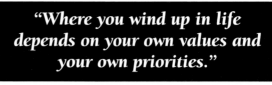

"Where you wind up in life depends on your own values and your own priorities."

Fully retired now for more than 25 years, L. Homer Surbeck can look back on a prestigious 50-year career in trial law, a field he once considered too controversial to be appropriate for a South Dakota preacher's son.

But this 1977 Horatio Alger Award winner doesn't spend much time looking back. He is busy with a wealth of activities, many of them centering on his wife, Margaret, whom he met and married at the age of 74. It is his first marriage. "When I had to work for a living, I was under pressure and never got around to getting married," he says. "Besides, I never met a woman with whom I had much in common, until I met Margaret. We have everything in common—funniest thing in the world."

Born in Minnesota, Surbeck was the son of a Prussian immigrant who became a small-town Presbyterian minister, then a church district superintendent in South Dakota. His mother was a self-taught country school teacher. Surbeck credits his parents for his lifelong commitment to hard work and honest effort.

Graduating from high school as valedictorian, Surbeck ignored an inner urge to become a lawyer and enrolled in an engineering course at the South Dakota School of Mines. But when he graduated in mining and metallurgy in 1924, he couldn't find a job. Finally, he decided to apply to law school and was awarded a scholarship to Yale. There, he edited the *Yale Law Journal* and graduated first in his class.

His success at Yale qualified him for a year as law secretary to the chief justice of the Supreme Court, William Howard Taft. "He was one of the greatest," says Surbeck. "And he was the one who finally convinced me that law was really for me."

After his year with Taft, Surbeck clerked with the New York firm of Hughes, Round, Schurman & Dwight, of which Charles Evans Hughes (later also chief justice of the Supreme Court) was a senior partner. Surbeck quickly developed into a top trial lawyer and became one of the nation's leading experts on antitrust law. Surbeck was made a partner in 1934. In his 50-year legal career, he participated in some of the most complex corporate legal cases and negotiations of the day.

For many years in retirement Surbeck enjoyed lecturing at retreats and seminars conducted by the Foundation for Christian Living, which was founded by Dr. Norman Vincent Peale. His theme always addressed the ways in which Christianity leads to a happier, more successful life. In 1986, Surbeck wrote a book called *The Success Formula That Really Works*, which was published by the foundation. "My book uses Solomon's formula, to put God first in everything you do, and He will direct you and crown your efforts with success," he says.

Of his Horatio Alger Award, Surbeck says, "It means a great deal to me to be a part of this honored group. I especially admire the work the Association is doing to help deserving young people receive a good education."

When Jessie Ternberg finished medical school at Washington University in the early 1950s, she wanted to serve her internship in surgery, but she soon learned hospitals were not accepting applications from women. She wrote to the head of the department at Washington University and told him what she thought of his policy.

Much to her surprise, the department chief agreed with her, abandoned the policy, and invited Ternberg to apply. Except for a stint in London, where she was trained in her specialty, pediatric surgery, she's been there ever since.

Ternberg's father deserted the family when she was a young girl. She was raised by her mother and grandmother in a small town in Minnesota. An $800 scholarship opened the door to college, and she enrolled at Grinnell, in Iowa, with the intention of becoming a lawyer.

By her junior year,

Ternberg realized her skills were in the sciences rather than law, and she began to think about medical school. She won a fellowship in biochemistry at the University of Texas. Later, she won a scholarship to Washington University's medical school in St. Louis, Missouri. By working summers in biochemistry, she was able to finance her education.

After completing an internship in Boston and a surgical residency in St. Louis, Ternberg joined the staff at the Washington University Medical Center as the only full-time surgeon at what was then the St. Louis Children's Hospital. For more than a decade, she performed as many as 500 operations a year, as well as treating others.

In 1972, thanks to her leadership, pediatric surgery became an official division of the medical center, and she was named to head that division. When she received her Horatio Alger Award in 1977, Ternberg was direc-

tor of pediatric surgery at Children's Hospital of Washington University. Today, Ternberg is professor emeritus of surgery and pediatrics.

Ternberg says her greatest contribution to society is taking care of children. To describe her philosophy of life, she uses a quote from Emerson: "To laugh often and much; to win the respect of honest critics and endure the betrayal of false friends; to appreciate beauty; to find the best in others; to leave the world a bit better whether by a healthy child, a garden patch, or a redeemed social condition; to know even one life has breathed easier because you have lived. This is to have succeeded."

Of her Horatio Alger Award, Ternberg says, "It is a high honor to be a part of this distinguished membership. I encourage the young Horatio Alger scholarship recipients to discover what they really like to do, then make the necessary effort to make their dreams reality."

JESSIE L. TERNBERG, M.D.

1977 Title
DIRECTOR, PEDIATRIC SURGERY
CHILDREN'S HOSPITAL OF
WASHINGTON UNIVERSITY

Current Title
PROFESSOR EMERITUS OF
SURGERY & PEDIATRICS
WASHINGTON UNIVERSITY
MEDICAL CENTER

> **"You can make your life whatever you want it to be."**

WALLY AMOS

1987 Title
FOUNDER & VICE CHAIRMAN
FAMOUS AMOS CHOCOLATE CHIP
COOKIE CORPORATION

Current Title
FOUNDER
UNCLE NONAME COOKIE
COMPANY

When Wally Amos won his Horatio Alger Award in 1987, his Famous Amos Chocolate Chip Cookie Corporation had made $12 million in annual sales with 35 Famous Amos stores throughout the United States and Asia.

It was a dream come true for Wally Amos, who had spent his childhood in poverty. At the age of 12, his parents divorced, and Amos was sent from his hometown in Tallahassee, Florida to live with his aunt and uncle in New York City. Five years later, he dropped out of high school and joined the Air Force, where he earned his high school equivalency certificate. Later, he worked in the mailroom at the William Morris Agency in New York, and within a year became the first black theatrical agent at William Morris. Eventually, Amos moved his family to Hollywood to start his own business as a personal manager for entertainment figures.

It was a struggle from the start. He never had a big star as a client, and he never seemed to have enough money to make ends meet. Finally, Amos took control of his life and began to earn a living doing something he had enjoyed doing since he was a child in his Aunt Della's kitchen—baking chocolate chip cookies.

He opened his first store in 1975 on Sunset Boulevard, with the help of investments made by show-business friends. His shop was an instant success. Soon, other Famous Amos shops began to appear.

But Amos' Horatio Alger story does not end there. In fact, he has lived the Horatio Alger story all over again. From 1985 to 1989, Amos was forced to sell his Famous Amos business four times to stabilize losses brought about by his own admitted mismanagement. By the time the fourth owner took over, Amos had no equity left in the business so he chose to leave it in 1989.

Amos started a new company in 1991 called Wally Amos Presents Chip and Cookie. But a year later, Famous Amos sued him, saying they owned his name and likeness. While that lawsuit was being pursued, Amos refused to accept defeat and started the Uncle Noname Company. "Noname," Amos says, "is pronounced no-nah-me, and is Hawaiian for 'temporary loss of legal name.'" The company, headquartered in Long Island, is doing well selling cookies, fat-free muffins, and fat-free pound cakes.

Amos wrote a book in 1994 about his experiences, calling it *The Man with No Name—Turn Lemons into Lemonade*. "I wanted people to know that you should not allow challenges to deter and defeat you," says Amos.

Amos published another book last year called *Watermelon Magic—Seeds of Wisdom, Slices of Life*. In it, Amos talks about choosing positive experiences and making positive decisions.

Today, Amos says his goal in life is to help people build self-esteem. "Most problems can be traced to low self-esteem," he says. "My purpose is to guide people to their inner strength and greatness. When people fill their lives with love, positive energy, faith, giving, and enthusiasm, they will be a success."

Amos is enthusiastic about his Horatio Alger Award, and is especially proud of the work being done to help the Horatio Alger scholars. "Horatio Alger gives these students a foundation of education, which in the end is a service to society. I am in awe of our scholars, and it is a privilege to be a part of this great Association."

JAMES A. COLLINS

CHAIRMAN &
CHIEF EXECUTIVE OFFICER
COLLINS FOODS
INTERNATIONAL, INC.

When Jim Collins, a young civil engineer, left his job to open a 19-cent hamburger stand in 1952, most of his friends just laughed at him.

"My old fraternity brothers from UCLA were all working for the big corporations," he says. "They'd come down during lunch, dressed in their suits and ties, and I'd be in the window, frying hamburgers. I guess they all thought I was a little crazy."

But Hamburger Handout, modeled after the first McDonald brothers' restaurant, grossed $420,000 its first year; and the doubters stopped laughing. Collins opened a second hamburger stand in 1957 and two more by 1959. In 1960, he added Kentucky Fried Chicken to his menu, and in 1962 he became the exclusive agent for Colonel Sanders in Southern California.

When Collins won his Horatio Alger Award in 1987, Collins Foods International had annual sales of more than $700 million. His company operated 201 Kentucky Fried Chicken stores in the U.S. and 54 in Australia. In addition, Collins Foods, a majority stockholder of Sizzler Restaurants International, Inc., operated or licensed 541 Sizzler Restaurants worldwide.

The son of an engineer who worked for Los Angeles County, Collins was 11 when his father built a house for the family. His father paid him 50 cents a day to help with the construction of the house. By the end of that summer, Collins had saved $40, which he used to buy a horse. To feed the horse, Collins and his father went to the Bank of America, where young Collins borrowed $45, and his father co-signed the loan. "I bought three tons of hay—enough to feed my horse for a year," Collins says. "Then I paid that money back out of my paper route."

That was only the beginning for the young entrepreneur. Collins joined a local 4-H Club, bought a cow, and sold milk to neighbors. He also sold turkeys at Thanksgiving, and mowed lawns for customers on his paper route. "I was a pretty busy kid," he laughs.

After high school, Collins joined the Navy, and served during World War II. He used the GI Bill to enroll at the University of California at Los Angeles. To help meet expenses, he washed dishes twice a day.

After leaving his job as a junior engineer, Collins opened Hamburger Handout in 1952. By 1960, Collins had four Hamburger Handout stands when he bought his first Kentucky Fried Chicken franchise. By 1968, Collins opened 240 chicken stores, and owned 25 of them. He also acquired 164 Sizzler Family Steakhouses.

Today, Collins is chairman of Sizzler International, Inc. He is especially proud of the company's expansion taking place in Australia and the Pacific Rim.

Collins teaches a class at UCLA's graduate school of management once a month, and reports "the opportunities for starting a business are greater now than ever, but first you should get a good education."

Collins says his Horatio Alger Award is a big honor. "It shows," he says "how I went from A to Z."

RAYMOND L. DANNER

1987 Title
CHAIRMAN
SHONEY'S, INC.

Current Title
CHIEF EXECUTIVE OFFICER
THE DANNER COMPANY

> **"If you want success, go out and work for it. You may get tired, but that's about the worst that can happen to you."**

At age 10, Raymond Danner made his first investment. He committed to spending $19.95 on a bicycle at Montgomery Ward by putting $3 down and paying $1 a month. The bike enabled young Danner to accept a summer job cutting overgrown lawns of repossessed houses owned by a Louisville savings and loan company. He made $1 per yard and by the end of that summer in 1935, Danner had paid off his bike and saved the rest of his earnings.

Born in Louisville, Kentucky, Danner was the son of a German immigrant who made his living as a paperhanger. Work was never plentiful for Danner's father, and after the stock-market crash of 1929, he rarely had work.

Danner and his parents lived in a room above a grocery store in a poor neighborhood of Louisville. The store was owned by his uncle, and four families lived above the store, each family having one room. Danner says the memory of those cramped years has been a strong motivator in his life.

When he was nine, his family moved to a small rented apartment. Six years later, Danner's father died. To help his mother, Danner had a paper route before school, worked at a local service station, and delivered groceries.

When he was 19, Danner joined the Army Air Corps as an aviation cadet. Danner came out of the service hoping to own his own business. He and a friend each invested $600 and bought an old, run-down store for $7,000. When they sold it 18 months later, they each pocketed $15,000. Danner used his profits to buy a franchise duckpin bowling alley for $12,000. One year later, he sold the franchise for $20,000.

After several other business ventures, Danner bought a Shoney's franchise in Nashville. By 1966, he operated seven Shoney's restaurants in the Nashville area. He expanded into other ventures, opening 22 Kentucky Fried Chicken franchises in Louisville. In 1969, he took his company public. Two years later, he merged his interests with Shoney's founder.

Danner was chairman of Shoney's when he received his Horatio Alger Award in 1987. There were 500 Shoney restaurants with annual revenues of $245 million. But in 1988, after 37 years with Shoney's, Danner chose to leave the company to pursue his own investment company full time. Today, the Danner Company includes three car dealerships and two manufacturing plants. For five years, his company built and owned a shrimp processing plant in China. Danner sold his interests in China and turned his attention to South America, where his interests include a logging company and waste disposal businesses.

Danner credits his concern for customer satisfaction for his business success. He encourages young people today to explore entrepreneurship, and advises them to discipline themselves to please their customers in whatever business they are in.

Of his Horatio Alger Award, Danner says, "I am honored to be a Horatio Alger Award recipient. My life story is a good example of what you can do if you have the desire to do it. I believe in what this award represents. I'm still making the American dream come true."

RUSSELL L. ISAACS

1987 Title
CHAIRMAN &
CHIEF EXECUTIVE OFFICER
HECK'S, INC.

Current Title
PARTNER
RUSSELL L. ISAACS & CO.

Born in Wheeling, West Virginia, the fifth child of a Welsh coal miner, Russell Isaacs never dreamed he would one day run a chain of department stores, or that he would work at the highest levels of state government. But Isaacs was not afraid of hard work and had within him an intense desire to succeed.

Still, it was not an easy beginning for Isaacs. His mother became ill when bearing her seventh child, which was stillborn. Isaacs and his siblings were sent to live with relatives until his mother died when he was seven. His father reunited his children in the tiny four-room house where Isaacs had been born. While their father worked long hours at the mine, the children took care of themselves and one another.

By age 12, Isaacs had started his own hauling business. "It may have been a hard life," says Isaacs today, "but I have no bad memories. We had love, we laughed a lot—I never thought about being poor."

In 1952, Isaacs joined the Marines and served in Korea. He used the GI Bill to enroll at West Virginia University, finishing a four-year accounting course in less than three years.

Upon graduation, Isaacs joined a Charleston accounting firm. Among the clients for whom he did tax work was Heck's, Inc., a fledgling chain of three discount department stores. In 1962, Heck's offered him a job as comptroller and treasurer. He joined the chain, and the following year was named to the company's board of directors. In 1969, he was responsible for Heck's becoming the first Charleston-based firm to be traded on the New York Stock Exchange.

Isaacs was named president of Heck's in 1973, and held that position until 1979. During his six-year tenure, company profits more than doubled. In 1979, Isaacs left the firm and joined a brokerage house as an executive vice president.

Three years later, Isaacs formed his own investment banking firm. At the same time, Heck's asked Isaacs to return as chairman of the board. He agreed and stayed with Heck's until 1987—the year he was inducted into the Horatio Alger Association.

Today, Isaacs serves on five boards and several executive committees for companies involved in manufacturing, distribution, construction, and banking.

An avid supporter of his native West Virginia, Isaacs has worked for the last five years with the West Virginia Basic Skills and Computer Education Foundation, which was formed by West Virginia's governor, the state school superintendent, and Isaacs. In addition, he is the first chairman of the West Virginia Infrastructure and Jobs Development Council, a panel designated to distribute state grants and loans for water, sewer, and infrastructure for economic development. He has been a key figure in securing economic development projects in West Virginia.

Reflecting on his success, Isaacs says, "Basically things don't change. You work hard, keep your nose clean, honor your teachers, obey your parents, and give something back." To him, success is being content with yourself. "I don't mean being complacent," he explains. "I mean feeling good about yourself and what you do."

Isaacs says, "There is a great deal of meaning to my Horatio Alger Award." He especially enjoys going to high schools in West Virginia to talk about the Horatio Alger scholarship program. "It's very rewarding to be with these young students. I thoroughly enjoy it."

"To accomplish something worthwhile, you have to persevere."

ARTHUR G. JAMES, M.D.

1987 Title
PROFESSOR OF SURGERY &
MEDICAL DIRECTOR
CANCER RESEARCH INSTITUTE
THE OHIO STATE UNIVERSITY

Current Title
EMERITUS MEDICAL DIRECTOR
A. G. JAMES CANCER HOSPITAL
& RESEARCH INSTITUTE
THE OHIO STATE UNIVERSITY

When Arthur James received his Horatio Alger Award in 1987, he was anxiously awaiting the completion of the $40 million Cancer Hospital and Research Institute on the campus of Ohio State University—a project that took him more than 30 years to bring to fruition. "It is," he says, "my greatest contribution to our community." The 160-bed institute is devoted entirely to the diagnosis and treatment of the cancer patient and to cancer research.

It's hard to believe that this gifted oncology surgeon once had doubts about being able to complete his education beyond high school. Born in a small coal-mining town in Ohio, he was the third child of Italian immigrant parents. James attended a two-room school in the mining camp where his father worked. When James was eight, his father left the mines to operate a grocery store. From that time on, James helped his parents with the store.

While admiring how hard his parents worked, young James understood that schooling was the key to a better life for him. An excellent student, James won a scholarship to Ohio State University in 1930. He earned his B.A., M.S., and M.D. degrees at the same

school, followed by internships at the University of Chicago Clinics and Duke University and a surgical residency at the Ohio State University Hospital. In 1942, he was accepted as a fellow in cancer training at Memorial Sloan-Kettering Cancer Center in New York City. However, he had to interrupt his training to serve in the Army during World War II. When the war ended, he completed his training, then returned to Ohio State as an assistant professor of surgery, specializing in oncology.

Throughout his career, James has been active in the American Cancer Society, and served as national president in 1972-1973. "The organization has done more than any other to acquaint the American public with the danger signals of cancer," he says. He was presented their highest award, the Medal of Honor, in 1990. James has also been active with the Society of Surgical Oncology, the Society of Head and Neck Surgeons, and the Columbus Surgical Society, serving as president of each.

When James won his Horatio Alger Award in 1987, he was the medical director of the Cancer Research Institute, which was renamed the Arthur G. James Cancer Hospital and

Research Institute in October 1987 to honor and recognize his work. He became the emeritus medical director and co-director of development in 1989. Over the past 10 years, he has been involved in all phases of the development of this cancer hospital, which opened in 1990. He has received many honors and awards for his accomplishments including the prestigious Ohio Governor's Award for medicine, Research, and Education in 1995, the Columbus Foundation's Outstanding Community Service Award in 1994, the Ohio Hospital Association's Meritorious Service Award in 1992, and the Ohio State University's Alumni Medalist Award in 1991.

James' philosophy of life is to embrace humanity. "Each of us has the capacity to help relieve human suffering, be it by a smile, a gift to the needy, the relief of pain by a physician, or the cure of a disease by a scientist," he says.

His Horatio Alger Award is especially prized because "it signifies my belief that if we persevere throughout life, we can achieve any goal. When you have a goal, and you know what you want to accomplish, then you just need to work hard, persevere, and stick with it."

> "There's a lot of hope in the unused elasticity of the individual."

Eugene Lang, son of an unemployed machinist, graduated from high school at the young age of 14. Waiting to enroll in the tuition-free City College system, he was working as a dishwasher in a New York restaurant when a regular restaurant patron, impressed by the youth's enterprise and ambition, arranged a full scholarship for him at prestigious Swarthmore College.

"You can never really repay anything like that," says Lang, now a prominent international businessman and philanthropist. "But it's part of life's circle that today I'm chairman emeritus of Swarthmore's board."

On June 25, 1981, it was clear that Lang never forgot the help that enabled him to get his Swarthmore education. On that day, he was the commencement speaker at P.S. 121, a Harlem elementary school from which he had graduated 53 years earlier. Facing a restless audience of 61 sixth graders, he realized that his planned speech about opportunity and the American dream would seem unrealistic. Instead, keying impromptu remarks to Martin Luther King's memorable dream, he concluded with this startling promise: "Stay in school and when you graduate from high school, I promise each

of you a scholarship so you can go on to college."

To sustain the incentive of this promise during the school years ahead, Lang constituted the P.S. 121 graduates as Dreamers of the first "I Have a Dream"® (IHAD) Project, and created an ongoing support and intervention program to encourage them to stay in school and qualify for college. Ten years ago, when Lang received his Horatio Alger Award, 54 of the original Dreamers were high school seniors of whom 49 earned their high school diplomas—a remarkable outcome considering the 75 percent-plus dropout rate for students in New York's inner-city communities. Today, Lang is still personally involved with his Dreamers. However, under the aegis of his "I Have a Dream"® Foundation, his East Harlem Project has grown into a nationwide confederation of more than 160 Projects in 61 cities with more than 15,000 Dreamers of whom about 2,500 have already enrolled in 283 colleges and universities.

The IHAD confederation continues to grow. Following Lang's model, Dreamers participate in year-round programs providing academic support, cultural exposures, and recreational activities, plus

an assured college opportunity. Project Sponsors personally get to know their Dreamers and help them define their dreams and work toward achieving them. "The core dynamic of IHAD," says Lang, "is the long-term caring relationship between sponsoring individuals and their Dreamers." Recognizing the nationwide impact of Lang's program, President Clinton presented him recently with this nation's highest civilian award, the Presidential Medal of Freedom.

After his early start on a degree at Swarthmore, Lang used his nights to earn a master's degree in business at Columbia University. Later, he studied mechanical engineering at Brooklyn Polytechnic Institute. In 1952, he founded REFAC Technology Development Corporation to help small high-tech companies establish their interests in foreign markets. Now a public company, REFAC is the world's largest single organization specializing in the negotiation and administration of international manufacturing licenses and joint ventures.

Lang says of his Horatio Alger Award, "It's very very special, representing the essence of America and its mandate, as a democracy, of an assured educational opportunity for every American."

EUGENE M. LANG

1987 Title
PRESIDENT
REFAC TECHNOLOGY

Current Title
CHAIRMAN
REFAC TECHNOLOGY
DEVELOPMENT CORPORATION

Founder and Chairman
"I HAVE A DREAM"
FOUNDATION®

> **"Know what you want to do, make sure it's right legally and morally, and go do it."**

MARSHALL
MANLEY

1987 Title
PRESIDENT &
CHIEF EXECUTIVE OFFICER
THE HOME GROUP

Current Title
CHAIRMAN
MANHATTAN ASSOCIATES

When Marshall Manley won his Horatio Alger Award in 1987, he was president and chief executive officer of The Home Group, Inc., which was financially troubled when he took office. With his new management approach, the company in one year went from losing $282 million to earning $229 million and continued during his tenure to set record earnings. Manley said at the time, "I like to build things, and I like to manage people." He does both very well.

Born in Newark, New Jersey, Manley lived with his parents and an uncle in the back of a candy store the family operated. When he was two, his father found a job as a machinist, and the family moved to a small apartment in Brooklyn. His mother worked at home typing envelopes while her son was young; then she found a full-time job. Young Manley helped the family by shining shoes on the boardwalk at Brighton Beach. Later, he sold ices from a pushcart and held a variety of other jobs, from delivering buttons in the garment district to being a stock boy in an art-supply store.

Although neither of his parents finished high school, there was never any doubt that Manley would get a good education. He attended Stuyvesant High School in Manhattan, a specialized school for college-bound students. After high school, he attended Brooklyn College and from there attended New York University, where he earned a law degree.

Manley joined a young California firm for his first job. He made partner within five years. From there, he joined Manatt, Phelps, Rothenberg, Manley and Tunney as a senior partner. In six years, he helped build it from six attorneys to a firm of 60.

His next move was as a founding partner of the California operations of Finley, Kumble, Wagner, Heine, Underberg, Manley, Meyerson & Casey. He was largely responsible for building that firm from 44 lawyers in 1978 to 600 in the mid-1980s.

In 1985, Manley took the position of president and chief executive officer of City Investing Company, a client, to manage the liquidation of that $8 billion company. When the liquidation was completed smoothly, he was elected president of The Home Group, Inc., and chairman of its financially troubled major subsidiary, Home Insurance Company.

Looking back on his successful career, Manley says, "I believe that to be successful, you have to reach your full potential in areas that are important to you, as opposed to those areas others decide are important to them."

In 1991, Manley left the corporate world and started his own business, Manhattan Associates. "I began to do transactions and evolved into a specialty I like, which is helping people create businesses. I bring relationships to them as well as expertise and experience. I get it off the ground and get it going," he says.

Today, Manley has more time to enjoy himself. Recently, he returned from participating in a cattle drive. He quips, "I sacrificed early so that I could enjoy myself later."

Of his Horatio Alger Award, Manley says, "It tells me how lucky I was. It gives me a better appreciation of getting the most out of life and doing the most I can for those in need."

1987 Award Recipient

Born in a poor rural area in the hills of Arkansas, Jerry Maulden was only five when he watched his father bid his family good-bye as he left to look for work during the final days of the Depression. His father found a job with the railroad, and several months later sent for his family. That was a traumatic experience for young Maulden, who was determined to work hard and be a success in life.

Just after Maulden's high school graduation, his father died. Determined to get a college education, Maulden enrolled at Little Rock Junior College, where he majored in accounting. He worked part time at a bakery and a local newspaper to pay his way. At the age of 19, Maulden married his high school sweetheart. Within two years, they had two children. Maulden switched to night school so that he could work full time. Eight years later, Maulden earned a degree in accounting.

One of Maulden's first jobs was as controller for Dillard Department Stores. In 1965, he joined Arkansas Power & Light Company as assistant to the treasurer and chief financial officer. Six years later, he went to the company headquarters in Little Rock as special assistant to the president and chief executive officer. He rose through the ranks quickly, serving as vice president, chief financial officer, treasurer, and secretary; and then as vice president, treasurer, and assistant secretary of the parent company.

In 1979, Maulden became president and chief executive officer of Middle South Services, Inc., a subsidiary of the parent company. Later that year, he was named president and chief executive officer of Arkansas Power & Light, which was having severe financial problems at the time.

Maulden reorganized the management, set new strategic directions, and instituted a structure based on management by objectives. Within five years, Arkansas Power & Light was turned around. When Maulden received his Horatio Alger Award in 1987, the company was recognized by an outside auditor as one of the best-managed electric utilities in the nation.

Since receiving his award, Maulden became president and chief operating officer of Entergy, the holding company for Arkansas Power & Light. Recently, he was elected vice chairman of the board of Entergy.

When he looks back over his successful career, Maulden says success is being happy and satisfied with yourself internally. "It's not being rich or heading a corporation that makes you successful. I'm talking about a life in which you are helping others, earning respect for what you contribute to society. This kind of success is available to people in all walks of life. It could be a teacher, a firefighter, or a CEO. To make it, you need good moral character, as good an education as you can get, and hard work. There is no substitute for it."

Of his Horatio Alger Award, Maulden says, "I am as proud of that award as any I've ever received. That one is special because of what the Association stands for—the focus on youth, and demonstrating that the American dream is still alive. In America, anyone can be successful regardless of how they started."

JERRY L. MAULDEN

1987 Title
PRESIDENT &
CHIEF EXECUTIVE OFFICER
ARKANSAS POWER & LIGHT CO.

Current Title
VICE CHAIRMAN OF THE BOARD
ENTERGY CORPORATION

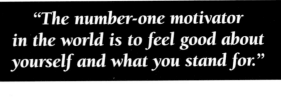

"The number-one motivator in the world is to feel good about yourself and what you stand for."

PATRICK G. RYAN

1987 Title
PRESIDENT &
CHIEF EXECUTIVE OFFICER
COMBINED INTERNATIONAL
CORPORATION

Current Title
CHAIRMAN &
CHIEF EXECUTIVE OFFICER
AON CORPORATION

When Patrick Ryan received his Horatio Alger Award in 1987, he was president and chief executive officer of Combined International Corporation, a broadly diversified insurance marketing organization that at the time had 15,000 employees and revenues of $2 billion. He came to that position through hard work and an entrepreneurial spirit that had always been a part of him. With that spirit, Aon has grown to a $4.5 billion company with more than 28,000 employees.

Born in Milwaukee, Wisconsin, Ryan was the son of a automobile dealer on the city's south side. Ryan and his six siblings attended a parochial elementary school. In high school, he worked at his father's dealership and on road construction gangs in the summers. He excelled at football and won an athletic scholarship to Northwestern University.

After 18 months at Northwestern, Ryan dropped out of football to please his parents, who were afraid he might be injured. To help pay his college expenses, he sold personalized college scrapbooks dorm-to-dorm. His enterprise earned him $8,000 in his senior year. "That business kindled my entrepreneurial sprit," Ryan says. "It convinced me I had the ability to develop a new business."

With a degree in finance and literature, Ryan turned his attention to finding a job in insurance. He joined Penn Mutual's Chicago office as a life insurance agent, but soon developed an idea he sold to the Continental Assurance Company of Chicago to offer insurance to auto dealerships' customers. In 1964, at the age of 26, he formed his own firm, Pat Ryan & Associates.

By 1968, Ryan's firm was selling $15 million in premiums a year. He took his firm public in 1971 to help raise capital to meet his long-range goal of diversify-

ing to multiple insurance products. In 1976, he acquired Globe Life and four insurance brokerage businesses. In 1981, he further expanded with the purchase of the James S. Kemper insurance agencies. In 1982, Ryan merged with Combined International and Combined Insurance Company of America.

Ryan says of his success, "I've moved relatively quickly in my career, but I've always tried to be patient and wait for the right time." Ryan encourages young people to choose a career carefully. "It's difficult to be successful at something you don't love," he says. He also encourages using a set of principles and standards to guide personal and professional conduct.

Of his Horatio Alger Award, Ryan says, "It means so much to me to be a part of this great organization. Helping young people receive a good education is especially rewarding to me."

138

Patrick G. Ryan

In Tribute

T he following are deceased members of this year's Anniversary Classes. Their past support for the Association and National Scholars is deeply appreciated.

1947

Walter S. Mack
President
Pepsi-Cola Company

Grover A. Whalen
New York Greeter and Businessman

Charles E. Wilson
President
General Electric

Robert R. Young
Chairman
New York
Central Railroad

1957

Charles C. Bales
Founder
C. C. Bales Agency

John Bentia
President
Alliance Manufacturing
Company

Thomas Carvel
President
The Carvel Company

Alwin F. Franz
Chairman of the Board and President
Colorado Fuel &
Iron Corporation

Joyce C. Hall
Founder
Hallmark Cards, Inc.

Gwilym A. Price
Chairman of the Board and President
Westinghouse Electric
Corporation

John J. Sheinin
President
Chicago Medical School

Harry Sugar
President
Alsco, Inc.

John H. Ware
Chairman of the Board
American Water
Works Company

Louis Zahn
President
Zahn Drug Co.

1967

Carl E. Anderson
Chairman & President
E. W. Bliss Company

Davre J. Davidson
Chairman of the Board
Automatic Retailers
of America

Ewing Marion Kauffman
President
Marion Laboratories, Inc.

Robert F. McCune
President
Robert F. McCune
Associates, Inc.

Lewis Phillips
President
Nedick's Store

Lawrence Welk
Conductor and Entertainer

1977

Robert P. Gerholz
President
Gerholz Community
Homes, Inc.

George J. Kneeland
Chairman and Chief Executive Officer
St. Regis Paper
Company

Roger Tory Peterson
Artist, Writer, Naturalist

Sarkes Tarzian
Founder and President
Sarkes Tarzian, Inc.

Danny Thomas
President
Danny Thomas
Productions, Inc.

Leadership

Association Members and Scholars

Our Members

A ll members are former recipients of the Horatio Alger Award. The dates and first titles are those of the year the Award was received. The second title is the member's current affiliation.

Aaron, Henry L. 1978
Baseball Player

Vice President
Turner Broadcasting

Abplanalp, Robert H. 1971
Chairman and President
Precision Valve Corporation

Allbritton, Joe L. 1994
Chairman of the Board
The Riggs National Bank of Washington, D.C.

Allumbaugh, Byron 1996
Chairman of the Board
Ralphs Grocery Company

Chairman of the Board, Retired
Ralphs Grocery Company

Amos, Wally 1987
Founder & Vice Chairman
The Famous Amos Chocolate Chip
Cookie Corporation

Founder
The Uncle Noname Cookie Company

Anderson, Carl E. (*) 1967
Chairman & President
E. W. Bliss Company

Anderson, Charles W. 1962
President
Ametek, Inc.

President, Retired
Ametek, Inc.

Anderson, Walter 1994
Editor
Parade Magazine

Andreas, Dwayne O. 1994
Chairman of the Board and Chief Executive
Archer Daniels Midland Company

Angelou, Dr. Maya 1992
Author/Professor

Anthony, Charles R. (*) 1963
Founder
C. R. Anthony Company

Antonini, Joseph E. 1993
Chairman, President and CEO
Kmart Corporation

Chairman, President and CEO, Retired
Kmart Corporation

Appley, Lawrence A. 1971
Chairman
American Management Association

Chairman Emeritus
American Management Association

Arboleya, Carlos J. 1976
President
Barnett Bank of South Florida

Vice Chairman, Retired
Barnett Bank of South Florida

142

Argyros, George L. 1993
Chairman and CEO
Arnel & Affiliates

Armour, Frank (*) 1960
President
H. J. Heinz Company

Ash, Mary Kay 1978
Chairman of the Board
Mary Kay Cosmetics, Inc.

Chairman Emeritus
Mary Kay Cosmetics, Inc.

Ash, Roy L. 1966
President
Litton Industries

Investor
Ash Capital

Athanas, Anthony 1978
President and Chief Executive Officer
Anthony's Pier Four, Inc.

Atkinson, Frank G. (*) 1962
President
Joseph Dixon Crucible Company

Autry, Gene 1964
Actor, Producer, and Businessman

Entertainer, Business and Baseball Executive

Babson, Roger W. (*) 1955
President
Babson's Statistical Service

Bailey, Frank (*) 1951
President
Title Guarantee & Trust Company

Bailey, William E. 1972
Chairman
Bestline Products, Inc.

Chairman of the Board
Direct Access Marketing, Inc.

Baker, Michael, Jr. (*) 1954
President
Michael Baker Corporation

Bales, Charles C. (*) 1957
Founder
C. C. Bales Agency

Barr, John Andrew (*) 1961
Chairman of the Board
Montgomery Ward & Co.

Baruch, Bernard M. (*) 1948
Financier

Bays, Karl D. (*) 1979
Chairman and CEO
American Hospital Supply Corporation

Beaver, Howard O., Jr. 1981
Chairman of the Board
Carpenter Technology Corporation

Chairman and CEO, Retired
Carpenter Technology Corporation

Beaver, Sandy (*) 1953
Chairman & President
Riverside Military Academy

Beebe, Kenneth (*)
Founder
Horatio Alger Awards Committee

Behlen, Walter D. (*) 1968
Chairman
Behlen Manufacturing Company

Benson, George Stuart (*) 1981
President Emeritus
Harding University

Benson, Ragnar (*) 1969
Chairman
Ragnar Benson, Inc.

Bentia, John (*)   1957
President
Alliance Manufacturing Company

Berdis, Albert J. (*)   1959
President
Great Lakes Steel Corporation

Berry, Loren M. (*)   1976
Founder
L. M. Berry & Company

Bickmore, Lee Smith (*)   1972
Chairman
Nabisco, Inc.

Block, John R.   1992
President
National-American Wholesale
Grocers' Association
President
Food Distributors International

Blumenthal, W. Michael   1980
Chairman and Chief Executive Officer
Burroughs Corporation

Limited Partner
Lazard Freres & Company

Bobst, Elmer Homes (*)   1965
Chairman
Warner-Lambert Pharmaceutical Co.

Boeckmann, Herbert F. II   1995
Owner/President
Galpin Motors, Inc.

Boehm, Helen F.   1975
Chairman
Edward Marshall Boehm, Inc.

Chairman of the Board/Owner
Boehm Porcelain Studio

Bongiovanni, Michael (*)   1979
President and CEO
Squibb Specialty Health Products Group

Bowles, John (*)   1963
President
Rexall Drug Company

Boyer, Ernest L. (*)   1990
President
The Carnegie Foundation for the
Advancement of Teaching

Brann, Donald R. (*)   1954
Directions Simplified, Inc.
Division of Easi-Bild Pattern Co., Inc.

Brennan, Walter (*)   1966
Actor

Brimmer, Andrew F.   1974
Board of Governors
Federal Reserve System

President
Brimmer and Company, Inc.

Brinker, Norman   1985
Chairman and CEO
Chili's Inc.

Chairman and CEO
Brinker International

Broad, Shepard   1979
Chairman of the Board
American Savings & Loan Association

Chairman, Retired
American Savings & Loan Association

Brooks, Benjy F.   1983
Professor & Chief of Pediatric Surgery
University of Texas

Senior Lecturer in Ethics and Leadership
University of Texas

Brown, Dorothy L   1994
General Surgeon
Clinical Professor of Surgery
Meharry Medical College

Brown, Jack H.   1992
Chairman of the Board
Stater Bros. Markets

Chairman, President & CEO
Stater Bros. Markets

Brown, Robert J.   1990
Founder, Chairman and President
B&C Associates, Inc.

Bruno, Joseph S. (*)   1980
Chairman of the Board
Bruno's, Inc.

Buchwald, Art   1989
Journalist/Author

Buck, Pearl S. (*)   1964
Author

Bunche, Ralph Johnson (*)   1952
U.S. Delegate to the United Nations

Bunting, Earl (*)   1948
Director
National Association of Manufacturers

Buntrock, Dean L.   1996
Chairman of the Board and Chief Executive Officer
WMX Technologies, Inc.

Burnett, Carol   1988
Comedienne & Actress

Entertainer

Burnett, Winston A.   1969
Chairman & President
Winston A. Burnett Company

Chairman and President
Winston A. Burnett Organization Ltd.

Burson, Harold   1986
Chairman of the Board
Burson-Marsteller

Founder/Chairman
Burson-Marsteller

Bush, John A. (*)   1954
Chairman of the Board
Brown Shoe Company

Byrd, Robert C.   1983
United States Senator from West Virginia
Minority Leader

United States Senator from West Virginia

Cain, Herman   1996
Chairman & Chief Executive Officer
Godfather's Pizza, Inc.

Caldwell, James R. (*)   1962
Chairman of the Board
Rubbermaid, Inc.

Cantu, Carlos H.   1997
President and CEO
ServiceMaster Company, L.P.

Camp, Wofford B. (*)   1978
Founder
W. B. Camp & Sons, Inc.

Caporella, Nick A.   1979
President & CEO
Burnup & Sims, Inc.

Chairman, President and CEO
National Beverage Corporation

Carlson, Chester (*)   1966
Inventor
Xerox Corporation

Carlson, Curtis L. 1979
President and Chairman of the Board
Carlson Companies, Inc.

Chairman and CEO
Carlson Companies, Inc.

Carlson, Edward E. (*) 1975
Chairman
UAL, Inc.

Carmichael, J. H. (*) 1958
Chairman
Capital Airlines

Carnahan, Paul (*) 1965
Chairman of the Board
National Steel Corporation

Carson, Benjamin S., Sr. 1994
Director of Pediatric Neurosurgery
The Johns Hopkins Hospital

Carter, Lester W. (*) 1956
President
American Hotel Association

Carvel, Thomas (*) 1957
President
The Carvel Company

Carver, Roy J. (*) 1976
Chairman and Founder
Bandag, Inc.

Cash, Johnny 1977
Entertainer

Castro, Bernard (*) 1963
President
Castro Convertible Corporation

Cathy, S. Truett 1989
Founder, Chairman & CEO
Chick-fil-A, Inc.

Chaddick, Harry F. (*) 1970
President
Chicago Industrial District, Inc.

Chandler, Marvin 1968
Chairman and President
Northern Illinois Gas Company

Chairman and President, Retired
Northern Illinois Gas Company

Chandler, R. Carl (*) 1965
Chairman
Standard Packaging Company

Clark, Catherine Taft (*) 1979
Founder
Brownberry Ovens, Inc.

Clark, Mary Higgins 1997
Author

Clayton, James L., Sr. 1991
Chairman, President and CEO
Clayton Homes, Inc.

Chairman & CEO
Clayton Homes, Inc.

Clements, W. W. "Foots" 1980
Chairman of the Board & CEO
Dr Pepper Company

Chairman Emeritus
Dr Pepper Company
Director
Dr Pepper/Seven-Up Companies, Inc.

Clements, William P., Jr. 1982
Governor
State of Texas

Former Governor
State of Texas

Coffman, Max   1967
President
Mammoth Mart, Inc.

Consultant
Coffman Realty, Inc.

Collier, David C.   1979
Group Vice President
General Motors Corporation

CEO, Operating Staffs, Retired
General Motors Corporation

Collins, Carr P. (*)   1964
Chairman
Fidelity Union Life Insurance Co.

Collins, James A.   1987
Chairman & CEO
Collins Food International, Inc.

Chairman
Sizzler International, Inc.

Connally, John B., Esq. (*)   1982
Former Governor of Texas
Former Secretary of the Treasury

Conti, Armando (*)   1956
President
Trenton Beverage Co.

Copley, Helen K.   1990
Chairman of the Corporation and CEO
Copley Newspapers

Courtelis, Alec P. (*)   1993
Chairman of the Board
Courtelis Company

Courtney, Thomas E. (*)   1950
President
Northern Illinois Corporation

Crandall, Robert L.   1997
Chairman and CEO
AMR Corporation/American Airlines, Inc.

Crean, John C.   1985
Chairman and CEO
Fleetwood Enterprises, Inc.

Crow, Trammell   1988
Founder & Chairman
Trammell Crow Company

Founder
Trammell Crow Company

Crowley, Mary C. (*)   1978
Founder and President
Home Interiors and Gifts, Inc.

Crown, Henry (*)   1953
President
Empire State Building and
Material Service Corporation

Cullen, Hugh R. (*)   1955
President
Quintana Petroleum Corporation

Culligan, Emmett J. (*)   1969
Founder
Culligan, Inc.

Cullum, George P., Sr. (*)   1974
Founder and Chairman of the Board
Cullum Construction Company

Cuomo, Mario M.   1985
Governor
State of New York

Former Governor
State of New York

D'Agostino, Nicholas, Sr. (*)   1982
Founder and Chairman of the Executive Committee
D'Agostino Supermarkets

Danner, Raymond L.   1987
Chairman
Shoney's, Inc.

Chief Executive Officer
The Danner Company

Davidson, Davre J. (*)   1967
Chairman of the Board
Automatic Retailers of America

Founder
ARA Services, Inc.

Davis, John W.   1990
Chairman of the Board, Retired
Dr Pepper Bottling Companies of Virginia

Dearden, William E. C.   1976
Vice Chairman and CEO
Hershey Foods Corporation

Chairman and CEO, Retired
Hershey Foods Corporation

Deaton, Charles   1969
Architect

DeBakey, Michael E.   1967
Chairman of Surgery
Baylor University

*Chancellor and Distinguished Service
Professor of Surgery*
Baylor College of Medicine

Dedman, Robert H.   1989
Founder and Chairman
Club Corporation International
Chairman
Franklin Federal Bancorp

Founder and Chairman
ClubCorp International

Dempsey, Jerry E.   1995
Chairman and CEO
PPG Industries, Inc.

DeVos, Richard M.   1996
Co-Founder and Former President
Amway Corporation

Dole, Robert J.   1988
*United States Senator from Kansas
Minority Leader*

Former Senate Majority Leader

Donlon, William J.   1993
Chairman and CEO
Niagara Mohawk Power Corporation

Chairman and CEO, Retired
Niagara Mohawk Power Corporation

Doolittle, James H. (*)   1972
Executive
Aviator & Insurance Company

Doran, Adron   1971
President
Morehead State University

President Emeritus
Morehead State University

Dorne, Albert (*)   1963
Artist, Illustrator and President
Famous Artists School

Dudley, Joe L., Sr.   1995
President and CEO
Dudley Products, Inc.

Dumont, Allen B. (*)   1949
President
Allen B. Dumont Laboratories

Ebbot, Percy J. (*)   1955
Vice Chairman
Chase Manhattan Bank of New York

Egan, Michael S.   1997
Chairman and CEO
Alamo Rent A Car, Inc.

Eisenhower, Dwight D. (*)   1961
Thirty-fourth President of the United States

Eisenhower, Milton S. (*)   1952
President
Pennsylvania State University

Ellis, Gilbert R. (*)   1978
Chairman of the Board
Household Finance Corporation

Ernsthausen, John F. (*)   1959
Founder & President
Norwalk Truck Lines, Inc.

Erving, Julius W.   1989
President
The Erving Group, Inc.

Ettinger, Richard Prentice (*)   1961
Chairman
Prentice-Hall, Inc.

Evans, Robert Beverley   1974
Detroit Industrialist; Director
American Motors Corporation

Chairman
Evans Industries, Inc.

Eyssell, Gustav S.   1956
President
Rockefeller Center, Inc.

President, Retired
Rockefeller Center, Inc.

Fairless, Benjamin F. (*)   1958
President
American Iron and Steel

Farber, Leonard L.   1985
Chairman of the Board
Leonard L. Farber Incorporated

Farley, William F.   1986
Chairman and Owner
Farley Industries

Chairman and CEO
Fruit of the Loom, Inc.

Farrell, Robert E.   1976
Co-Founder & President
Farrell's Ice Cream Parlour Restaurants

Chairman Emeritus
Pacific Coast Restaurant, Inc.

Fertel, Ruth   1995
Founder and Chairman of the Board
Ruth's Chris Steak House

Finley, Clarence C.   1978
Corporate Group Vice President
Burlington Industries, Inc.

Corporate Group Vice President, Retired
Burlington Industries, Inc.

Fisher, John E.   1993
General Chairman
Nationwide Insurance Companies

General Chairman, Retired
Nationwide Insurance Enterprise

Fisher, Zachary   1990
Partner
Fisher Brothers
Founder
Intrepid Sea-Air-Space Museum

Flaherty, Lee F.   1979
Founder and President
Flair Communications Agency, Inc.

Chairman and CEO
Flair Communications Agency, Inc.

Fleming, Sam M.   1970
President
Third National Bank and NLT Corporation

Chairman, Retired
Third National Bank

Fogarty, Robert (*)   1971
Founder and President
Habitation Resources, Inc.

Fong, Hiram L. 1970
United States Senator from Hawaii
United States Senate

Chairman of the Board
Finance Enterprises, Ltd.

Ford, Gerald R., Jr. 1983
Thirty-eighth President of the United States

Foreman, George 1984
Minister
Church of the Lord Jesus Christ

Minister/Professional Boxer

Foresman, R. J. (*) 1975
President
Michigan General Corporation

Foster, T. Jack (*) 1964
Building and Land Developer

Foster, William F. (*) 1966
President
Merit Clothing Company

Franz, Alwin F. (*) 1957
Chairman of the Board and President
Colorado Fuel & Iron Corporation

Fuller, Alfred C. (*) 1959
The Original "Fuller Brush Man"

Fuller, Walter D. (*) 1953
Chairman of the Board and President
Curtis Publishing Company

Fuqua, J. B. 1984
Chairman and CEO
Fuqua Industries, Inc.

Chairman of the Board
The Fuqua Companies

Galbreath, John W. (*) 1960
Realtor, Owner
John W. Galbreath & Co.

Gellman, Allen B. (*) 1956
President
Elgin-American Company

Gerholz, Robert P. (*) 1977
President
Gerholz Community Homes, Inc.

Giles, Terry M. 1994
President
Giles Enterprises

Goldberg, Arthur J. (*) 1968
*Permanent Representative of the
United States to the United Nations*

Grace, William E. 1966
President and Chief Executive Officer
Fruehauf Corporation

President and CEO
Sassy Enterprises

Graham, Billy 1965
Evangelist, Author, and Educator
Billy Graham Evangelistic Association

Gramm, Phil 1991
United States Senator from Texas

Gray, Byron A. (*) 1953
Chairman
International Shoe Company

Gray, Harry J. 1984
Chairman of the Board, Retired
United Technologies Corporation

Managing General Partner, Investment Fund
Harry Gray, Mel Klein & Partners, L.P.,
Principal, Harry Gray Associates

Gray, Helen M. (*) 1982
Honorary Member, Executive Director
Horatio Alger Association of
Distinguished Americans, Inc.

Greenberg, Alan "Ace"   1997
Chairman
Bear Stearns

Grimes, Warren G. (*)   1961
Chairman of the Board
Grimes Manufacturing Company

Grundhofer, John "Jack"   1997
Chairman, President, & CEO
First Bank System, Inc.

Guida, Peter M.   1981
Professor of Surgery
Cornell University Medical College
Chief of the Frank Glenn Division of Surgery
New York Hospital

Professor of Surgery
Cornell University Medical College
Attending Surgeon, New York Hospital

Haffa, Titus (*)   1963
Chairman
Webcor, Inc.

Haggai, Thomas S.   1980
President and CEO
Tom Haggai & Associates, Inc.

Chairman and CEO
IGA, Inc.

Haggar, J. M., Sr. (*)   1976
Founder & Honorary Chairman
Haggar Company

Halas, George S. (*)   1968
Owner & Coach
Chicago Bears Football Club

Halbouty, Michel T.   1978
Consulting Geologist and Petroleum Engineer

Chairman and CEO
Michel T. Halbouty Energy Co.

Hall, Joyce C. (*)   1957
Founder
Hallmark Cards, Inc.

Hallauer, Carl S. (*)   1960
President and Chairman of the Board
Bausch and Lomb Optical Company

Hamid, George A. (*)   1948
Owner
Atlantic City Steel Pier

Hammell, Alfred L. (*)   1959
President
Railway Express Agency, Inc.

Hansen, Zenon C.R. (*)   1974
Chairman and President
Mack Trucks, Inc.

Harburg, E. Y. (*)   1979
Lyricist, Writer, & Lecturer

Hardy, Alexander G. (*)   1971
Chairman
The AVEMCO Group

Harken, Thomas L.   1992
Chairman
Harken and Associates

Chairman of the Board & CEO
Tom Harken & Associates, Inc.

Harman, Leon W.   1971
President
Harman Managers Investment, Inc.

Chairman of the Board
Harman Management Corporation

Harris, Alexander (*)   1950
President
Ronson Corporation

Harris, J. Ira 1977
General Partner
Salomon Brothers

General Partner
Lazard Freres and Company

Hart, Ralph A. (*) 1994
Chairman of the Board, Retired
Heublein, Inc.

Harvey, Paul 1983
News Commentator
ABC Network

Commentator
Paul Harvey News

Hawkinson, Robert Wayne (*) 1966
President
Belden Manufacturing Corporation

Herenton, Willie W. 1988
Superintendent
Memphis City School System

Mayor
City of Memphis, Tennessee

Hershey, John O. 1981
Chairman and President
Milton Hershey School

Chairman and President, Retired
Milton Hershey School

Hickel, Walter J. 1972
Governor of Alaska

Former Governor of Alaska

Hill, James M. (*) 1962
Hill Enterprises

Hilton, Conrad N. (*) 1950
Founder & President
Hilton Hotels Corporation

Hirshhorn, Joseph H. (*) 1976
Entrepreneur and Art Collector
Joseph H. Hirshhorn Foundation

Hite, Morris L. (*) 1980
Chairman and President
Allcom, Inc.

Hodges, Luther H. (*) 1970
Chairman
Research Triangle Foundation

Hoffman, Paul Gray (*) 1953
Chairman
Studebaker-Packard Corporation

Hood, Clifford F. (*) 1954
President
United States Steel Corporation

Hoover, Herbert C. (*) 1953
Thirty-first President of the United States

Hope, Bob 1968
Entertainer

Hopkins, John Jay (*) 1953
Chairman and President
General Dynamics Corporation

Horrigan, Edward A., Jr. 1981
Executive Vice President
R. J. Reynolds Industries, Inc.
Chairman and Chief Executive Officer
R. J. Reynolds Tobacco Company

Chairman
Balmoral Investments, Inc.

Howard, John A. 1967
President
Rockford College

President, The Ingersoll Foundation
Counselor, The Rockford Institute

Hughes, Paula D. (*)   1984
First Vice President-Director
Thomson McKinnon Securities, Inc.

Huizenga, H. Wayne   1992
Chairman & CEO
Blockbuster Entertainment Corporation

Chairman
Huizenga Holdings, Inc.

Hulme, Milton G. (*)   1958
President
Hulme, Applegate & Huphrey, Inc.

Huntsman, Jon M.   1997
Chairman and CEO
Huntsman Corporation

Hurley, Roy T. (*)   1956
President
Curtiss-Wright Company

Hutchings, James L.   1990
Chairman of the Board
S&H Fabricating & Engineering, Inc.

Imperatore, Arthur E.   1982
Chairman of the Board and President
A-P-A Transport Corporation

Chairman and Chief Executive Officer
A-P-A Transport Corporation

Inouye, Daniel K.   1989
United States Senator from Hawaii

Isaacs, Russell L.   1987
Chairman & CEO
Heck's Inc.

Partner
Russell L. Isaacs & Co.

Jacobs, Walter L. (*)   1959
President
The Hertz Corporation

James, Arthur G.   1987
Professor of Surgery & Medical Director
Cancer Research Institute
Ohio State University Hospital

Professor Emeritus
Department of Surgery
Ohio State University

James, Daniel, Jr. (*)   1976
Commander in Chief
North American Air Defense Command

Jannetta, Peter J.   1990
Chairman, Neurological Surgery
University of Pittsburgh
School of Medicine

Walter E. Dandy Professor & Chairman
Department of Neurological Surgery
University of Pittsburgh
School of Medicine

Jeffers, Dean. W.   1975
General Chairman and CEO
The Nationwide Insurance Organization

General Chairman and CEO, Retired
Nationwide Insurance Companies

Jenkins, George W. (*)   1966
President
Publix Supermarkets, Inc.

Jennings, Waylon   1988
Entertainer

Owner/President
WGJ Productions, Inc.

Johnson, E. Ellis (*)   1964
President
Chicago, Rock Island and Pacific Railroad

Johnson, George E. 1981
President & Chairman of the Board
Johnson Products Co., Inc.

Chairman, Indecorp, Inc.
Consultant and Retired Chairman,
Johnson Products Company, Inc.

Johnson, Henry A. 1985
President & CEO
Spiegel, Inc.

President
Henry A. Johnson & Associates, Inc.

Johnson, Herbert C. (*) 1974
Chairman
Consolidated Natural Gas Company

Johnson, John H. 1966
President & Editor
Johnson Publishing Company, Inc.

Chairman, CEO and Publisher
Johnson Publishing Company, Inc.

Johnson, Rafer L. 1981
Vice President, Community Affairs
Continental Telephone Service Corporation
Olympic Gold & Silver Medalist

Chairman of the Board
California Special Olympics

Johnson, W. Thomas 1988
Publisher and Chief Executive Officer
Los Angeles Times
Vice Chairman
The Times Mirror Company

President
CNN

Johnson, Wallace E. (*) 1968
President
Holiday Inns of America, Inc.

Johnston, Wayne A. (*) 1963
President
Illinois Central Railroad

Jones, James Earl 1997
Actor

Jones, Quincy 1995
Chief Executive Officer
Qwest Records

Jonsson, J. Erik (*) 1969
Mayor
City of Dallas, Texas

Jorgensen, Earle M. 1984
Chairman of the Board & CEO
Earle M. Jorgensen Company

Chairman Emeritus
Earle M. Jorgensen Company

Joyce, John M. (*) 1956
President
"Seven-Up" Bottling Company

Karcher, Carl N. 1979
Founder, Chairman of the Board & CEO
Carl Karcher Enterprises, Inc.

Founder and Chairman Emeritus
CKE Restaurants

Karnes, William G. 1961
President
Beatrice Foods Company

Chairman and President, Retired
Beatrice Foods Company

Katz, Joseph M. (*) 1981
Chairman of the Board
Papercraft Corporation

Kauffman, Ewing Marion (*) 1967
President
Marion Laboratories, Inc.

Kelce, Merl C. (*)   1961
President
Peabody Coal Company

Kelly, Dee J.   1995
Senior Founding Partner
Kelly, Hart & Hallman, P.C.

Kelly, Patrick C.   1997
Chairman and CEO
Physician Sales & Service, Inc.

Kemp, Jack   1993
Former Secretary
U.S. Department of Housing and
Urban Development

Co-Director
Empower America

Kemp, John D.   1991
Chief Executive Officer
United Cerebral Palsy Associations

President & CEO
Very Special Arts

Keough, Donald R.   1988
President, Chief Operating Officer & Director
The Coca-Cola Company

Chairman
Allen & Company Incorporated

Kerrigan, James J. (*)   1952
Chairman of the Executive Committee
Merck & Company

Kettering, Charles F. (*)   1952
Research Consultant
General Motors Corporation

Kincaid, Garvice David (*)   1960
Financier
Bankers and Securities, Inc.

King, Kenneth J., Sr. (*)   1968
President
Kenny King's Family Restaurants

Kirsner, Joseph B.   1979
*Louis Block Distinguished Service
Professor of Medicine*
The University of Chicago Hospitals and Clinics

Kissinger, Henry A.   1992
Chairman
Kissinger Associates, Inc.

Klein, Melvyn N.   1996
President and Chief Executive Officer
JAKK Holding Corporation
Managing General Partner
GKH Partners, L.P.

Kneeland, George J. (*)   1977
Chairman and Chief Executive Officer
St. Regis Paper Company

Knowlton, Richard L.   1992
Chairman, President & Chief Executive Officer
Geo. A. Hormel & Company

Chairman
The Hormel Foundation

Kraft, James L. (*)   1951
Chairman
Kraft-Phoenix Cheese Corporation

Kroc, Ray A. (*)   1972
Founder and Chairman
McDonald's Corporation

Kroll, Alex   1993
Chairman and CEO
Young & Rubicam, Inc.

Chairman Emeritus
Young & Rubicam, Inc.

LaLanne, Jack   1979
President & Owner
The Jack LaLanne Company

Lecturer, Author, TV Personality
Befit Enterprises

Landry, Thomas W.   1983
Head Coach
Dallas Cowboys

President
Landry Investment Group

Lang, Eugene M.   1987
President
REFAC Technology Development Corporation

Chairman
REFAC Technology Development Corporation
Founder and Chairman
"I Have a Dream" Foundation

Lannan, J. Patrick (*)   1962
Chairman
Susquehanna Corporation

Lawson, Fred A. (*)   1954
President
E.L. Patch Company

Lay, Herman Warden (*)   1969
Chairman
PepsiCo, Inc.

Leach, Edward C., Sr. (*)   1960
President
Jack Tar Hotels

Lear, William P. (*)   1954
Chairman
Lear, Inc.

Lesher, Richard L.   1980
President
Chamber of Commerce of the United States

Leverone, Nathaniel (*)   1964
Chairman
Automatic Canteen Company of America

Levinson, Samuel H. (*)   1966
President
Railweight, Inc.

Levis, William E. (*)   1955
Chairman
Owens-Illinois Glass Company

Lewyt, Alexander M. (*)   1950
Inventor
Lewyt Vacuum Cleaner

Ling, James, J.   1962
President
Ling-Temco-Vought, Inc.

President
Empiric Energy, Inc.

Linkletter, Art   1976
Chairman
Linkletter Enterprises

Little, Bernie, Sr.   1994
Chairman
Bernie Little Distributors, Inc.

Love, Ruth B.   1983
General Superintendent of Schools
Chicago Board of Education

Distinguished Professor & Coordinator
San Francisco State University

Lubin, Charles W. (*)   1968
Founder and Chairman
Kitchens of Sara Lee

Luce, Clare Boothe (*)   1974
*Playwright, Actress, Former Congresswoman,
Former Ambassador, and Lecturer*

Luckman, Charles   1948
Pereira and Luckman

Chairman and CEO
The Luckman Management Company

Ludden, Allen (*)   1962
Senior Executive and College Bowl Moderator
CBS

Lyet, J. Paul (*)   1983
Former Chairman
Sperry Corporation

MacArthur, John D. (*)   1961
Owner
Bankers Life & Casualty Company

Mack, Walter S. (*)   1947
President
Pepsi-Cola Company

Maddy, Joseph E. (*)   1965
National Music Corporation

Magnus, Finn H. (*)   1951
President
Magnus Harmonica Corporation

Mahoney, David J.   1977
Chairman & President
Norton Simon, Inc.

Chairman
The Charles A. Dana Foundation

Manley, Marshall   1987
President and CEO
The Home Group, Inc.

Chairman
Lincoln Terrace Capital Corp.

Marcus, Ben   1982
Chairman of the Board & CEO
The Marcus Corporation

Founder
The Marcus Corporation

Marcus, Bernard   1993
Founder, Chairman and Chief Executive Officer
The Home Depot

Mardikian, George M. (*)   1976
Food Consultant and Owner
Omar Khayyam's Restaurant

Marotta, Vincent G.   1975
President
North American Systems, Inc.

President
Marotta Corporation

Marovitz, Abraham Lincoln   1979
Senior United States District Court Judge
Northern District of Illinois

Marriott, J. Willard (*)   1974
Founder & Chairman of the Board
Marriott Corporation

Marshall, Thurgood (*)   1969
Associate Justice
United States Supreme Court

Marusi, Augustine R.   1981
Director and Chairman of the Executive Committee
Borden, Inc.

Chairman of the Board, Retired
Borden, Inc.

Maulden, Jerry L.   1987
President & Chief Executive Officer
Arkansas Power & Light Company

President & COO
Entergy Corporation

McAfee, James W. (*)   1955
President
Union Electric Co.

McCain, Warren E.   1991
Chairman of the Board &
Chief Executive Officer, Retired
Albertson's Inc.

McCall, Abner V. (*)   1963
President
Baylor University

McConnell, John H. 1983
Chairman and CEO
Worthington Industries, Inc.

Chairman and Founder
Worthington Industries, Inc.

McCune, Robert F. (*) 1967
President
Robert F. McCune Associates, Inc.

McKee, Charles A. 1981
Chairman & CEO
Electrolux Corporation
Executive Vice President
Consolidated Foods Corporation

Chairman & CEO, Retired
Electrolux Corp.
Executive Vice President, Retired
Sara Lee

McKenna, Andrew J. 1993
President
Schwarz Paper Company

Chairman, President & CEO
Schwarz Paper Company

McKuen, Rod 1976
Poet, Composer, Author, and Singer

Founder
Rod McKuen Enterprises

McMahon, Ed 1984
Television Performer

Founder
McMahon Communications, Inc.

Menk, Louis W. 1978
Chairman & CEO
Burlington Northern, Inc.

Chairman
Black Mountain Gas Co.

Merlo, Harry A. 1980
Chairman and President
Louisiana-Pacific Corporation

President
Merlo Corporation

Milano, John 1976
President
The Byer-Rolnick Company

President
Milano Hat Company, Inc.

Millsop, Thomas E. (*) 1952
President
National Steel Corporation

Mitchell, George J. 1990
United States Senator from Maine
Majority Leader

Special Council
Verner, Liipfert, Bernhard, McPherson, and Hand

Mitchell, George P. 1984
Chairman and President
Mitchell Energy & Development Corp.

Chairman and CEO
Mitchell Energy & Development Corp.

Mitchell, James P. (*) 1959
United States Secretary of Labor

Moffett, James R. 1990
Chairman of the Board and CEO
Freeport-McMoRan Inc.

Chairman of the Board and CEO
Freeport-McMoRan Copper & Gold Inc.

Moll, Clarence R. 1962
President
Pennsylvania Military College

President Emeritus
Widener University

Monaghan, Thomas S. 1986
President & Chairman of the Board
Domino's Pizza, Inc.

President
Domino's Pizza, Inc.

Moore, Gordon E. 1996
Chairman of the Board
Intel Corporation

Moore, Thomas W. 1968
Group Vice President
American Broadcasting Company, Inc.

President Emeritus
ABC Television Network
Vineyard Owner

Moran, Jim 1996
Founder & Chairman of the Board
JM Family Enterprises, Inc.

Mortel, Rodrigue 1985
University Professor and Chairman
Department of Obstetrics and Gynecology
Pennsylvania State University College of Medicine

Associate Dean & Director
Pennsylvania State University
Cancer Center

Morton, Azie Taylor 1979
Thirty-sixth Treasurer of the United States

Director of Marketing
GRW Capital Corporation

Motley, Arthur H. (*) 1974
Chairman
Parade Sunday Magazine

Mott, Charles Stewart (*) 1971
Director
General Motors Corporation
Founder
The Mott Foundation

Muntz, Earl W. (*) 1949
President
Muntz T.V., Inc.

Musial, Stan 1991
Baseball Hall of Famer

Nadeau, Lee E. (*) 1949
President
The Nestle-Le Muir Company

Nance, James J. (*) 1951
Chairman
First Union Real Estate Investments

Neff, Francine I. 1976
Thirty-fifth Treasurer of the United States

Founder
Neff & Company

Neubauer, Joseph 1994
Chairman & CEO
ARA Services

Chairman and CEO
ARAMARK Corporation

Neuharth, Allen H. 1975
President & CEO
Gannett Company, Inc.

Chairman
The Freedom Forum

Nicholas, Frank C. 1979
Chairman of the Board & President
Beech-Nut Foods Corp.

President, Chairman & CEO, Retired
Beech-Nut Foods Corp.

Nidetch, Jean 1989
Founder
Weight Watchers International, Inc.

Founder and Consultant
Weight Watchers International, Inc.

Nodyne, George O. (*)   1963
President
East River Savings Bank of New York

Noyes, Charles F. (*)   1959
President
Charles F. Noyes Company, Inc.

O'Brien, Gerald C. (*)   1969
President and Chairman of the Board
North American Development Corp.

O'Connor, John J.   1981
President
Miami National Bank

President, Retired
Miami National Bank

O'Green, Fred W.   1983
Chairman & CEO
Litton Industries, Inc.

Chairman Emeritus
Litton Industries, Inc.

O'Malley, Patrick L.   1972
President
Canteen Corporation

Chairman Emeritus
Canteen Corporation

Odlum, Floyd (*)   1972
Financier

Ornelas, Louise Herrington   1996
Co-Founder
TCA Cable, Inc.

Pappajohn, John   1995
President
Equity Dynamics, Inc.

Patterson, William A. (*)   1965
President
United Airlines

Paulson, Allen E.   1985
Chairman, President & CEO
Gulfstream Aerospace Corporation

Chairman
Gulfstream Aerospace Corporation

Paulucci, Jeno F.   1965
Chairman of the Board & President
Chun King Corporation

Chairman, President & CEO
Luigino's Inc.

Payne, William T. (*)   1958
Founder
Big Chief Drilling Co.

Peale, Norman Vincent (*)   1952
Editor-in-Chief and Publisher
Guideposts
Co-Founder, Foundation for Christian Living
Co-Founder, Peale Center

Peale, Ruth Stafford   1977
Author, Lecturer and Publisher

Editor-in-Chief and Publisher
Guideposts
Co-Founder, Peale Center

Penney, J. C. (*)   1953
Founder
J. C. Penney Company

Perot, H. Ross   1972
Chairman
Electronic Data Systems Corporation

Chairman
Perot Systems Corporation

Perry, Russell H. (*)   1981
Chairman of the Board and CEO
Republic Financial Services, Inc.

Person, Ann   1977
Founder and President
Stretch & Sew, Inc.

President/Owner
Stretch & Sew, Inc.

Peterson, Roger Tory (*)   1977
Artist, Ornithologist & Author

Phillips, Lewis (*)   1967
President
Nedick's Store

Pierson, Elmer F. (*)   1966
President and Chairman
The Vendo Company

Pilliod, Charles J., Jr.   1982
Chairman of the Board & CEO
The Goodyear Tire & Rubber Co.

Chairman
Dal Tile International

Pohlad, Carl R.   1989
President
Bank Shares, Inc. & Marquette Bank Minneapolis

President
Marquette Bancshares, Inc.

Poling, Daniel A. (*)   1954
Editor
Christian Herald

Poling, Harold A.   1991
Chairman and CEO
Ford Motor Company

Chairman of the Board, Retired
Ford Motor Company

Portman, John C., Jr.   1990
Chairman and CEO
The Portman Companies

Chairman
Portman Holdings

Powell, Colin L.   1991
Chairman
Joint Chiefs of Staff
Department of Defense

Former Chairman
Joint Chiefs of Staff

Presley, W. Dewey   1968
President
First National Bank of Dallas

President, Retired
First International Bancshares, Inc.

Price, Gwilym A. (*)   1957
Chairman of the Board and President
Westinghouse Electric Corporation

Price, James R. (*)   1972
Chairman of the Board
National Homes Corporation

Rachunis, Michael L. (*)   1969
Eye, Ear, Nose & Throat Specialist

Rackley, Frank B. (*)   1955
President
Jessup Steel Company

Rasmussen, Wallace N.   1978
Chairman & CEO
Beatrice Foods

Chairman, Retired
Beatrice Foods

Reagan, Ronald   1969
Governor
State of California

Fortieth President of the United States

Reinhart, D. B. (*)   1989
Owner, Chairman and CEO
Gateway Foods, Inc.

Resnick, Frank E. (*)   1988
President & CEO
Phillip Morris, U.S.A.

161

Reston, James B. (*) 1972
Vice President
The New York Times

Revson, Charles (*) 1950
Chairman of the Board & President
Revlon Corporation

Rice, Robert L. 1975
Founder & Chairman of the Board
Health Industries, Inc.

President & CEO
Spa Fitness Centers, Inc.

Richards, Gilbert F. (*) 1980
Chairman of the Board & Consultant
The Budd Company

Chairman and CEO, Retired
The Budd Company

Richards, Harold J. (*) 1970
Chairman of the Board
Fidelity Corporation

Rickenbacker, Edward V. (*) 1956
Chairman of the Board and President
Eastern Airlines

Riggio, Vincent (*) 1949
Chairman of the Board
American Tobacco Company

Riklis, Meshulam 1969
Chairman of the Board
McCrory Corporation

Roach, John V. 1990
Chairman of the Board and CEO
Tandy Corporation

Robbie, Joseph (*) 1979
President and Owner
Miami Dolphins

Roberts, William A. (*) 1952
President
Allis-Chalmers Manufacturing Company

Robey, Margaret Durham (*) 1968
President
Southern Seminary and Junior College

Robin, Albert A. 1991
Founder & President
The Robin Construction Company

Founder
The Robin Construction Company

Robinson, Eddie 1988
Football Coach/Athletic Director
Grambling State University

Football Coach
Grambling State University

Roderick, David M. 1988
Chairman and CEO
USX Corporation

Chairman and CEO, Retired
USX Corporation

Rodriguez, Juan "Chi Chi" 1986
Professional Golfer

Rogers, Kenny 1990
Singer/Entertainer
Kenny Rogers Productions

Rogers, Ralph B. 1986
Chairman of the Board
Texas Industries, Inc.

Rollins, John W., Sr. 1963
President
Rollins Leasing Corporation

Chairman and CEO
Rollins Truck Leasing Corp. and
Rollins Environmental Services, Inc.

Rollins, O. Wayne (*) 1986
Chairman and Chief Executive Officer
Rollins, Inc. & Rollins Communications, Inc.

Rosen, Samuel (*) 1978
Emeritus Clinical Professor of Otolaryngology
Mt. Sinai School of Medicine

Rosenberg, Anna (*) 1949
Assistant Secretary
Department of Defense

Rouse, James W. (*) 1992
Founder
The Enterprise Foundation

Royal, Darrell 1996
*Special Assistant to the President
for Athletic Programs*
The University of Texas at Austin

Rubloff, Arthur (*) 1955
Chairman of the Board
Arthur Rubloff and Company

Rusk, Howard A. (*) 1971
Director
Institute of Rehabilitation Medicine

Russell, Frank C. (*) 1951
President
The F. C. Russell Company

Russell, Herman J. 1991
Chief Executive Officer
H. J. Russell & Company

Chairman and CEO
H. J. Russell & Company

Ryan, Patrick G. 1987
President and CEO
Combined International Corporation

President and CEO
Aon Corporation

Ryan, T. Claude (*) 1958
President
Ryan Aeronautical Co.

Ryder, James A. 1960
President
Ryder Systems, Inc.

Chairman
Automotive Answer, Inc.

Salatich, William G. 1975
President
Gillette North America

President
William G. Salatich Consulting, Inc.

Salvati, Raymond E. (*) 1958
President
Island Creek Coal Company

Sampson, Robert G. 1980
Vice President, Office of the Chairman
United Airlines

Vice President/Special Assistant, Retired
Office of the Chairman, United Airlines

Sanders, Harland (*) 1965
Founder
Kentucky Fried Chicken Corporation

Sarnoff, David (*) 1951
Chairman
Radio Corporation of America

Sax, George D. (*) 1965
Chairman
Exchange National Bank

Schafer, Harold L. 1953
President
Gold Seal Company

Founder, Theodore Roosevelt Medora Foundation
Founder/Owner, Gold Seal Company

Scheie, Harold G. (*) 1974
Founder
Scheie Eye Institute

Schuller, Robert H. 1989
Founder and Senior Pastor
The Crystal Cathedral

Founder and Senior Pastor
Crystal Cathedral Ministries

Schwartz, Robert G. 1994
Chairman, President and CEO, Retired
Metropolitan Life Insurance Company

Scotese, Peter G. 1981
Vice Chairman
Springs Mills, Inc.

Chief Executive Officer, Retired
Springs Industries, Inc.

Scott, Charles R. 1984
President & CEO
Intermark, Inc.

Chief Executive Officer
The Executive Committee

Scott, Walter, Jr. 1997
Chairman and President
Peter Kiewit Sons', Inc.

Self, James C. (*) 1955
President
Greenwood Mills

SerVaas, Beurt R. 1980
Chairman
Curtis Publishing Company

Chairman
SerVaas, Inc.

Sharp, Carl J. (*) 1955
Chairman of the Board
Acme Steel Company

Shaver, Dorothy (*) 1948
President
Lord & Taylor

Shea, Andrew R. (*) 1954
President
Pan American Grace Airlines

Shearing, George A. 1978
Pianist, Arranger, and Composer

Sheinin, John J. (*) 1957
President
Chicago Medical School

Shepherd, Mark, Jr. 1984
Chairman of the Board & CEO
Texas Instruments Incorporated

General Director
Texas Instruments Incorporated

Shinn, George 1975
President
George Shinn & Associates

Chairman of the Board, Shinn Enterprises, Inc.

Shoemaker, William L. 1978
Professional Jockey

Professional Jockey, Retired

Shorts, R. Perry (*) 1963
Chairman of the Board
Second National Bank of Saginaw

Shula, Don   1995
Head Coach
Miami Dolphins

Don Shula's Hotel & Golf Resort

Silber, John   1992
President
Boston University
Chancellor
Boston University

Sims, Riley V. (*)   1970
Chairman of the Board
Burnup & Sims, Inc.

Slater, John H. (*)   1960
Owner and President
Slater Food Service Management

Small, Rose Cook   1977
Founder and Vice President
Bluebird, Inc.

Smith, C. R. (*)   1961
Founder
American Airlines

Smith, Deen Day   1993
Chairman of the Board
Cecil B. Day Investment Company

Smith, Donald S. (*)   1955
President
Perfection Stove Company

Smith, George V.   1982
President and Owner
Smith Pipe & Supply, Inc.

Smith, Harold V. (*)   1954
President
Home Insurance Company

Snyder, W. Cordes, Jr. (*)   1956
President
Blaw-Knox Manufacturing Company

Solinsky, Robert S. (*)   1960
President and Chairman
National Can Corporation

Sollenbarger, Lee R.   1980
Chairman of the Board
Transcon Lines

Chairman of the Board, Retired
Transcon, Inc.

Solomon, Joseph (*)   1978
Senior Partner
Lehman, Rohrlich & Solomon

Spanos, Alex G.   1982
Chairman of the Board
A. G. Spanos Enterprises, Inc.

Chairman, A. G. Spanos Companies
Chairman/Owner, San Diego Chargers

Sparks, Jack D. (*)   1985
Chairman, President and CEO
Whirlpool Corporation

Spoor, William H.   1986
Chairman Emeritus
The Pillsbury Company

Stargell, Willie   1983
Former Team Captain
Pittsburgh Pirates

Baseball Consultant
Pittsburgh Pirates

Stassen, Harold E.   1951
Special Assistant to President Eisenhower

Statesman, Author
Former Governor of Minnesota

Steinfeld, Manfred 1981
Co-Founder, Chairman and CEO
Shelby Williams Industries

Chairman
Shelby Williams Industries

Stephens, Jackson T., Sr. 1980
Chairman of the Board & CEO
Stephens Inc.

Chairman of the Board
Stephens Inc.

Stiefel, Herbert J. (*) 1975
President
Stiefel/Raymond Advertising, Inc.

Stokes, Carl B. (*) 1970
Mayor
City of Cleveland, Ohio

Stone, Edward Durell (*) 1971
Architect

Stone, Norman H. (*) 1974
Founder, Chairman and CEO
Stone Container Corporation

Stone, W. Clement 1963
President
Combined Insurance Company of America

Chairman Emeritus
Aon Corporation

Sugar, Harry (*) 1957
President
Alsco, Inc.

Sunnen, Joseph (*) 1954
President
Sunnen Products Company

Surbeck, L. Homer 1977
Partner
Hughes, Hubbard, & Reed

Wall Street Attorney, Retired

Tabler, William B., Sr. 1958
Architect

Owner
William B. Tabler Architects

Tarzian, Sarkes (*) 1977
Founder and President
Sarkes Tarzian, Inc.

Taylor, Patrick F. 1986
Chairman of the Board & President
Taylor Energy Company

Chairman, CEO and President
Taylor Energy Company

Ternberg, Jessie L. 1977
Director of Surgery, Pediatric Division
St. Louis Children's Hospital

Professor Emeritus of Surgery & Pediatrics
Washington University Medical Center

Thayer, Paul 1982
Chairman of the Board & CEO
The LTV Corporation

Chairman of the Executive Committee
Computerbase International, Inc.

Thomas, Clarence 1992
Associate Justice
United States Supreme Court

Thomas, Danny (*) 1977
President
Danny Thomas Productions, Inc.

Thomas, Edwin J. (*) 1962
Chairman and Chief Executive Officer
Goodyear Tire & Rubber Co.

Thomas, Lowell (*)   1971
Commentator and Author

Thomas, R. David   1979
Founder and Chairman
Wendy's International, Inc.

Founder and Senior Chairman of the Board
Wendy's International, Inc.

Thornton, Charles B. (*)   1964
Founder and Chairman of the Board
Litton Industries

Timan, Joseph (*)   1968
President
Horizon Land Corporation

Tippie, Henry B.   1996
*Chairman of the Executive Committee and
Vice Chairman of the Board*
Rollins Truck Leasing Corporation

Toppel, Harold   1966
Chairman of the Board
H. C. Bohack Company, Inc.

Chairman Emeritus
Pueblo International

Trout, Monroe E.   1995
Chairman Emeritus
American Healthcare Systems

Trump, Fred C.   1985
Chairman of the Board
The Trump Organization

Tuohy, Walter J. (*)   1961
President
Chesapeake and Ohio Railway

Turner, Arthur E.   1981
Chairman of the Board of Trustees
Northwood Institute

Founder
Northwood University

Turner, Basil S.   1981
Director & Consultant
CTS Corporation

Chairman of the Board, Retired
CTS Corporation

Turner, Fred L.   1991
*Senior Chairman,
Chairman of the Executive Committee*
McDonald's Corporation

Turner, R. E.   1997
Vice Chairman
Time Warner, Inc.

VanCaspel Harris, Venita   1982
President & Owner
VanCaspel & Company

Founder and CEO
VanCaspel & Co., Inc.

Ventres, Romeo J.   1989
Chairman of the Board & Chief Executive Officer
Borden, Inc.

Chairman and CEO, Retired
Borden, Inc.

Viscardi, Henry, Jr.   1983
Founder and President Emeritus
Human Resources Center

Founder and President Emeritus
National Center for Disability Services

Volid, Peter (*)   1958
Chairman of the Board
King Korn Trading Stamp Company

Vosburgh, Louis S. (*)   1965
Chairman of the Board
Lincoln Extension Institute

Waldron, Hicks B. *Chairman of the Board and CEO* Avon Products, Inc. *Chairman* Boardroom Consultants, Inc.	1985	**Watt, Herbert J. (*)** *President* Peabody Institute	1964
Walker, Eric A. (*) *President* Pennsylvania State University	1959	**Weisenberger, Arthur (*)** *President* Arthur Weisenberger, Inc.	1951
Walter, Henry G. (*) *Honorary Trustee* Illinois Masonic Medical Center	1972	**Welk, Lawrence (*)** *Conductor and Entertainer*	1967
Walter, James W., Sr. *President* Jim Walter Corporation *President* Waltsons, Inc.	1961	**Welsh, Leslie T. (*)** *President* Leslie T. Welsh, Inc.	1984
		Whalen, Grover A. (*) *New York Greeter and Businessman*	1947
Walton, Sam M. (*) *Chairman and Chief Executive Officer* Wal-Mart Stores, Inc.	1984	**Whitaker, Frederic (*)** *Founder* Audubon Artists	1974
Ware, John H. (*) *Chairman of the Board* American Water Works Company	1957	**White, Edward A.** *President* Bowmar Instrument Corporation *Chairman* Bowmar Instrument Corporation	1962
Warner, John C. (*) *President* Carnegie Institute of Technology	1964	**Wilkinson, Ernest L. (*)** *President Emeritus* Brigham Young University	1976
Warp, Harold (*) *Founder* Flex-O-Glass, Inc.	1979	**Williams, Jackie** *Chairman of the Board & Chief Executive Officer* AAA Enterprises, Inc. *Chairman of the Board* Jackie Williams, Ltd.	1970
Washington, Dennis R. *Chairman* Washington Corporations	1995	**Wilson, Charles E. (*)** *President* General Electric	1947
Watson, Thomas J. (*) *Chairman of the Board* International Business Machines	1953		

Wilson, Huey, J. 1981
Founder and Chairman of the Board
H. J. Wilson Company, Inc.

Founder and Chairman
Huey Wilson Interests

Wilson, Kemmons 1970
Chairman of the Board
Holiday Inns, Inc.

Chairman
Kemmons Wilson Companies

Winfrey, Oprah 1993
Chairman and Chief Executive Officer
Harpo Entertainment Group and
Harpo Productions, Inc.

Winokur, Harry 1965
Founder and Chairman of the Board
Mister Donut of America

Winter, Elmer L. 1967
President
Manpower, Inc.

President, Retired
Manpower, Inc.

Wooten, Benjamin H. (*) 1959
President
First National Bank of Dallas

Worthington, Leslie B. 1966
President
U.S. Steel Corporation

President, Retired
U.S. Steel Corporation

Wyly, Sam 1970
Chairman of the Board
University Computing Company

Chairman
Sterling Software Inc. and Michael's Stores, Inc.

Yamasaki, Minoru (*) 1964
Architect
Minoru Yamasaki & Associates

Yeager, Charles E. 1986
Brigadier General (Retired)
United States Air Force
President
Yeager, Inc.

Young, Adam 1957
President
Young Television Corporation
Vice Chairman and Treasurer
Adam Young, Inc.

Treasurer
Young Broadcasting, Inc.

Young, Robert R. (*) 1947
Chairman
New York Central Railroad

Zahn, Louis (*) 1957
President
Zahn Drug Co.

Zukor, Adolph (*) 1953
Chairman
Paramount Pictures Corporation

Horatio Alger National Scholars 1984-1997

ALABAMA

Dallas, Shauna	Le Flore High School of Communications and Arts, Mobile	1997
Rush, Stephanie	Fairhope High School, Fairhope	1997
Forsyth, Erick	W. P. Davidson High School, Mobile	1996
Garner, Shannon	Robertsdale High School, Robertsdale	1996
Hammons, Shana	Hanceville High School, Hanceville	1995
Norwood, Stormy	Citronelle High School, Citronelle	1995
Frank, Erica	Foley High School, Foley	1994
Lestelle, Chris	Theodore High School, Theodore	1994
Grubb, Michele	Baker High School, Mobile	1993
Lam, Tony	Alba High School, La Batre	1992
Mims, Melvia	Ben C. Rains High School, Mobile	1991
Singletary, Christopher	J. O. Johnson High School, Huntsville	1991
Lake, Joel	Tuscaloosa County High School, Tuscaloosa	1990

ALASKA

Kuth, Summer	Tok High School, Tok	1997
Wood, Lilith	Petersburg High School, Petersburg	1996
Ramsay, Dale	Sitka High School, Sitka	1995
Armour, Celis	Bartlett High School, Ft. Richardson	1994
Ner, Arvin	Ketchikan High School, Ketchikan	1993
Nichols, Sara	Susan B. English School, Seldovia	1993
Oscar, Thomas	Paul T. Albert Memorial High School, Tununak	1992
Tulik, Paul	Paul T. Albert Memorial High School, Tununak	1992
Keller, Regina	Bethel Regional High School, Bethel	1991
Paul, Karen	Kwigillingok High School, Kwigillingok	1990
Hoover, Elaine	Akula Elitnaurvik High School, Kasigluk	1989

ARIZONA

Lewis, Sarah	Yuma High School, Yuma	1997
Phair III, James	Chandler High School, Chandler	1997
Abdullah, Hawwah	Agua Fria High School, Avondale	1996
Beltran, Christopher	Nogales High School, Nogales	1996
Bejarano, Adelita	Tempe High School, Tempe	1995
Hubbard, Pilar	Coronado High School, Scottsdale	1994
Heyer, Autumn	Flowing Wells High School, Flowing Wells	1993
Hanley, Lisa	Mesa High School, Mesa	1992
Ussery, Loretta	Shadow Mountain High School, Shadow Mountain	1991
Rowe, Lisa	Chandler High School, Chandler	1990
Cutler, Renee	Sahuaro High School, Tucson	1988
Browne, Timothy	Sahuaro High School, Tucson	1986

ARKANSAS

Evans, Curt	Crossett High School, Crossett	1997
Newcom, Karen	Marion High School, Marion	1997
Coleman, Karissa	Camden-Fairview High School, Camden	1996
Staten, Thomas	Jonesboro High School, Jonesboro	1996
Elcan, Clint	Harrison High School, Harrison	1995
Iverson, Pamela	Magnolia High School, Magnolia	1995
Minteer, Carey	North Pulaski High School, Jacksonville	1994
Goff, David	Springdale High School, Springdale	1993
Daniels, Karla	Arkadelphia High School, Arkadelphia	1992
Frey, Mari	White Hall High School, White Hall	1991
Cornell, Staci	Northside High School, Fort Smith	1990

CALIFORNIA

Lara, Guadalupe	Woodlake High School, Woodlake	1997
Lopez, Miguel	Healdsburg High School, Healdsburg	1997
Aguilar, Olvin	San Marcos High School, San Marcos	1996
Le Beaux, Akeida	Mt. Diablo High School, Concord	1996
Ramey, Chris	Oroville High School, Oroville	1996
Labra, Veronica	Ukiah High School, Ukiah	1995
Merlo, Jay	El Camino High School, Sacramento	1995
Noriega, Arcelia	University High School, Irvine	1994
Philbrick, Rose	Livermore High School, Livermore	1994
Billimoria, Dimple	Eureka High School, Eureka	1993
Poth, Brian	Tulare Union High School, Tulare	1993
Wiederhold, Sarah	Oakmont High School, Roseville	1993
Love, Terrence	Colton High School, Colton	1992
Lopez, Alfred	Roosevelt High School, Clarksville	1991
Roberts, Tammy	Redlands High School, Redlands	1991
Mojica, Aurelia	Chico High School, Chico	1990
Leiker, Randy	Banning High School, Wilmington	1989

Rodriguez, Louis	Hesperia High School, Hesperia	1989
Ly, Anh	Belmont High School, Los Angeles	1988
Dale, Beverly	Livermore High School, Livermore	1987
Evelyn, Reyna	Hesperia High School, Hesperia	1987
Svalstad, Christy	Fountain Valley High School, Fountain Valley	1986
Cavanna, Christina	Livermore High School, Livermore	1985
Sanchez, Manuel	Belmont High School, Los Angeles	1985
Schreiber, Jeffrey	Beverly Hills High School, Beverly Hills	1984

COLORADO

Forssberg, Mandy	Las Animas High School, Las Animas	1997
Legg, Mary Grace	Lincoln High School, Denver	1997
Frazier, Keo	Aurora Central High School, Aurora	1996
Moores, Ray	Gateway High School, Gateway	1996
Alirez, Adam	Greeley Central High School, Greeley	1995
Wallen, Sabrina	Fountain-Ft. Carson High School, Fountain	1995
Vigil, Tania	Pueblo County High School, Pueblo	1994
Vidal, Shelli	Aspen High School, Aspen	1993
Ash, Tangala	Montbello High School, Denver	1992
Heukels, Michael	Broomfield High School, Broomfield	1991
Hyslop, Scott	Arapahoe High School, Littleton	1990
Kerekes, Kevin	Arapahoe High School, Littleton	1990

CONNECTICUT

Jackson, Kenya	Manchester High School, Manchester	1997
Ng'andu, Jennifer	New London High School, New London	1997
Lutzky, Alexander	Joel Barlow High School, West Redding	1996
White, Jennifer	Weaver High School, Hartford	1995
Rivera, Manuel	Warren Harding High School, Bridgeport	1994
DeLeo, Debbie	East Hartford High School, East Hartford	1993
Santiago, Alex	Bulkeley High School, Hartford	1992
Muller, Marissa	E. O. Smith High School, Storrs	1991
Thiele, Mary	Fairfield High School, Fairfield	1990
Acevedo, Hector	T. S. Weaver High School, Hartford	1989

DELAWARE

Fischer, Cheryl	Dover High School, Dover	1997
Gibson, Jonathan	Sussex Central High School, Georgetown	1997
Bender, Mike	Lake Forest High School, Felton	1996
Carothers, Christin	Seaford High School, Seaford	1996
Layton, Caesar	Milford High School, Milford	1995
Marlette, Dawn	Laurel Senior High School, Laurel	1994
Fader, Mary	Ursuline Academy, Wilmington	1993
Hawthorne, Brian	Cape Henlopen High School, Lewes	1993
Hassler, Kellie	Caesar-Rodney High School, Camden	1992
Kehnast, William	Middletown High School, Middletown	1991
Taylor, Celeste	Brandywine High School, Wilmington	1990

DISTRICT OF COLUMBIA

Berrios, Cristina	Cardozo Senior High School, Washington	1997
McCoy, Theresa	Eastern Senior High School, Washington	1997
Robinson, Edward	School Without Walls, Washington	1996
Thomas, Maudie	Anacostia High School, Washington	1995
Hill, Shareem	Benjamin-Banneker High School, Washington	1994
Henderson, Tertia	F. W. Ballou High School, Washington	1993
Lockie, Adrienne	Wilson High School, Washington	1992
Prince, Dione	William McKinley High School, Washington	1991
Chew, Karen	Paul L. Dunbar High School, Washington	1990
Horton, Paul	Woodson High School, Washington	1989
Sanders, Sophia	Roosevelt High School, Washington	1989
Tate, Pasquelo	Eastern High School, Washington	1988

FLORIDA

Alexa, Heidi	St. Cloud High School, St. Cloud	1997
Larimore, Kate	Osceola High School, Kissimmee	1997
Roman, Julio	Miami Springs Senior High School, Miami Springs	1996
Salazar, Cynthia	Pahokee Middle Senior High School, Pahokee	1996
Flood, Jamillah	Hallandale High School, Hallandale	1995
Williams, Roger	Glades Central High School, Belle Glade	1995
Bowditch, Sherri	Largo High School, Largo	1994
Connell, Chris	Leon County High School, Tallahassee	1994
Dayan, Hillit	Northeast High School, Oakland Park	1993
St. Louis, Alinx	Coral Park Senior High School, Miami	1993
Benson, Shawn	Palm Bay High School, Melbourne	1992
McRae, Cecelia	Orange Park High School, Orange Park	1991
Simmons, Jamal	Paxon High School, Jacksonville	1991
Hines, Kimberly	Ely High School, Pompano Beach	1990
Mize, Sean	Killian High School, Miami	1989
Formoso, Margaret	South Plantation High School, Plantation	1988
Kohl, Pamela	Forest Hill High School, Palm Beach	1988
Mouw, Jamie	Lake Brantley High School, Altamonte Springs	1988
Ohmstede, David	Brandon High School, Brandon	1987
Schneider, Linda	Osceola High School, Kissimmee	1987
Kustin, Adam	J. P. Taravella High School, Coral Springs	1986
Soltren, Sally	Lake Brantley High School, Altamonte Springs	1986
Buehler, Elizabeth	Brandon High School, Brandon	1985

GEORGIA

Reid, Yvonne	Harlem High School, Harlem	1997
Spivak, Kathleen	McEachern High School, Powder Springs	1997
Dodd, Matt	Valwood School, Valdosta	1996
Gotel, Doug	Jasper County High School, Monticello	1996
Keith, John	East Coweta High School, Sharpsburg	1995
Lee, Kris	Winder-Barrow High School, Winder	1995
Durden, Torarie	Cook High School, Adel	1994
Harris, Jackie	Washington-Wilkes Comp. High School, Washington	1994
Jackson, Tracey	B. E. Mays High School, Atlanta	1993
Reeves, Matt	Joseph T. Walker School, Marietta	1993

Kitchens, Scott	Davidson Fine Arts School, Augusta	1992
Scales, Sandi	Elbert County Comp High School, Elbertson	1991
Fritz, Laura	Marietta High School, Marietta	1990
Amos, Clifton	McEachern High School, Powder Springs	1989
May, Nelson	Towers High School, Decatur	1987
Bachman, Andrew	John McEachern High School, Powder Springs	1986
Cain, Richard	Towers High School, Decatur	1985

HAWAII

Kim, Krystal	Governor Wallace Rider Farrington High School, Honolulu	1997
Matayoshi, Leilani	James B. Castle High School, Kaneohe	1997
Sherman, Jennifer	Waipahu High School, Waipahu	1996
Thorpe, Farren	Waiakea High School, Hilo	1995
Eslit, Christine	Radford High School, Honolulu	1994
Li, Margaret	Moanalua High School, Honolulu	1993
Hercules, Tiffini	Kalaheo High School, Kailua	1992
Renaud, Jeffrey	Kahuku High School, Kahuku	1991
Lam, Anmay	Kailua High School, Kailua	1990

IDAHO

Ariwite, December	Blackfoot High School, Fort Hall	1997
Follett, Tracy	Bonneville High School, Idaho Falls	1997
Davidson, Cynthia	Lake City High School, Coeur d'Alene	1996
Nielsen, Hyrum	Hillcrest High School, Idaho Falls	1996
Daniel, Jeremiah	Weiser High School, Weiser	1995
Winward, Mathew	Preston High School, Preston	1994
Meza, Florence	Skyline High School, Idaho Falls	1993
Jensen, Amber	Minico High School, Minico	1992
Meacham, Manuel	Declo High School, Declo	1991
Roberts, Jennifer	Rimrock Jr./Sr. High School, Bruneau	1990

ILLINOIS

Bit-Ivan, Esther	Mather High School, Chicago	1997
Dekelaita, Nina	Mather High School, Chicago	1997
Frank, Josh	Knoxville High School, Knoxville	1996
Hines, Kim	Martin Luther King Jr. High School, Chicago	1996
Roberson, Darius	Martin Luther King Jr. High School, Chicago	1996
Bonner, Paula	Sacred Heart-Griffin High School, Springfield	1995
Conner, Tiffany	Hyde Park Career Academy, Chicago	1995
Stewart, LaVern	Hyde Park Career Academy, Chicago	1995
Brubaker, James	Rantoul Twp High School, Rantoul	1994
Velez, Rachel	Madonna High School, Chicago	1994
Gulino, Robert	Gordon Technical High School, Chicago	1993
Jaimes, Patricia	McHenry High School, McHenry	1993
Harris, Michelle	Newton Community High School, Newton	1992
Moran, Christy	Effingham High School, Effingham	1991
Mini, Dawn	Lyons Township High School, LaGrange	1990
Carreras, Antoinette	Rich Central High School, Olympia Fields	1989
Riess, Jana	Galesburg High School, Galesburg	1987
Wilson, Lynne	Hyde Park Career Academy, Chicago	1987

Endter, Laureen	Downers Grove North High School, Downers Grove	1986
Palacio, Luz	Waukegan East High School, Waukegan	1986
Brunswick, Amy	Mattoon High School, Mattoon	1985

INDIANA

Sutton, Demetrius	William Henry Harrison High School, Evansville	1997
Saragoza, Philip	South Dearborn High School, Aurora	1996
Wilkinson, Chad	Washington Alternative High School, Terre Haute	1996
Simpson, Janet	Arsenal Technical High School, Indianapolis	1995
Spaetti, Adam	North High School, Evansville	1995
Johnson, April	North Side High School, Ft. Wayne	1994
Kamper, Heather	Floyd Central High School, Floyds Knobs	1994
Ngo, Danny	North Virgo High School, Terre Haute	1993
Richardson, Alesha	Wirt High School, Gary	1992
Kinnaird, Holly	William Henry Harrison High School, Evansville	1991
Kahl, Joanna	Arlington High School, Indianapolis	1990
Elliott, Katherine	Merrillville Senior High School, Merrillville	1988
McIntosh, Melissa	Connersville Senior High School, Connersville	1988

IOWA

Hall, Melanie	Glidden-Ralston Community School District, Glidden	1997
Girsch, Mike	Northern University High School, Cedar Falls	1996
Pearce, Matt	Eldora-New Providence High School, Eldora	1996
Johnston, Jill	Indianola High School, Indianola	1995
Poling, Leah	Gilbert Community High School, Gilbert	1995
Tuttle, Denise	Chariton High School, Chariton	1993
Segebart, Janna	Denison High School, Denison	1992
McNally, Tony	Fredericksburg High School, Fredericksburg	1991
Miller, Teresa	East High School, Des Moines	1990
Smeins, Shawn	Parkersburg High School, Parkersburg	1986

JAMAICA

Gooden, Michelia	Herbert Morrison Technical High School, Montego Bay	1997
Brooks, Carla	Herbert Morrison Technical High School, Montego Bay	1996

KANSAS

Adcox, Christi	McLouth High School, McLouth	1997
Fuchs, Kimberly	Shawnee Mission North High School, Merriam	1997
Davies, Jeff	Hiawatha High School, Hiawatha	1996
Schmelzle, Willie	Valley Falls High School, Valley Falls	1996
Hicks, Cassie	Hoxie High School, Hoxie	1995
Wallace, Melinda	Hesston High School, Hesston	1995
Heaton, Denise	Hugoton High School, Hugoton	1994
Greenough, Jolene	Uniontown High School, Uniontown	1993
Habluetzel, Chad	Blue Valley North High School, Overland Park	1992

| Miller, Amy | Pittsburgh High School, Pittsburgh | 1991 |
| Ernst, Matthew | Russell High School, Russell | 1990 |

KENTUCKY

Cooper, Maryfrances	Rowan County Senior High School, Morehead	1997
Eads, Mona	Madison Southern High School, Berea	1997
Coffey, Marcia	Rockcastle County High School, Mount Vernon	1996
Miller, Amanda	Greenwood High School, Bowling Green	1996
Denney, Melissa	Wayne County High School, Monticello	1995
Keene, Bridgette	Pikeville High School, Pikeville	1995
Bayless, Jennifer	Greenup County High School, Greenup	1994
Fries, Melissa	South Laurel High School, London	1993
Lopez, Beatriz	Fort Knox High School, Fort Knox	1992
McCubbin, Judy	Hart County High School, Munfordville	1991
Hand, Rebecca	Western High School, Louisville	1990
Bays, Earl	Paintsville High School, Paintsville	1988
Wells, Margery	Ohio County High School, Hartford	1988

LOUISIANA

Barton, Ashley	Grant High School, Dry Prong	1997
Daigle, Katie	Thibodaux High School, Thibodaux	1997
Brown, Doug	Captain Shreve High School, Shreveport	1996
Durisseau, Jamieka	Lake Charles-Boston High School, Lake Charles	1996
Landry, Kerii	Northside High School, Lafayette	1995
Steele, Jonathan	Grace King High School, Metairie	1995
Harris, Jennifer	LaSalle High School, Olla	1994
Tilley, Patricia	Bishop Sullivan Catholic High School, Baton Rouge	1994
Wilson, Xavier	Francis T. Nicholls High School, New Orleans	1993
Hernandez, Maria	O. Perry Walker High School, New Orleans	1992
Hall, Keith	Menard High School, Alexandria	1991
Eastlack, Robert	Lafayette High School, Lafayette	1990
Ethridge, Robin	St. Mary's Dominican High School, New Orleans	1987
Pinto, Christopher	Holy Cross High School, New Orleans	1987
Michelli, Jamie	Grace King High School, Metairie	1985

MAINE

Hussey, Shannon	Biddeford High School, Biddeford	1997
Muyderman, Dovid	Portland High School, Portland	1997
Pass, Tia	Erskine Academy, Augusta	1996
Payeur, Keri	Westbrook High School, Westbrook	1995
Linscott, Cathy	Bonny Eagle High School, Standish	1994
Sherman, Kelley	Brewer High School, Brewer	1993
Lufkin, Stephanie	Old Town High School, Old Town	1992
Perreault, Donna	Community High School, Fort Kent	1991
Kubeck, Brian	Calais High School, Calais	1990
Blake, Gloria	Westbrook High School, Westbrook	1989

MARYLAND

Basharyar, Leema	Seneca Valley High School, Germantown	1997
Masimore, Kristi	North Carroll High School, Hampstead	1997
Fike, Danelle	Northern Garrett County High School, Accident	1996
Sewell, Katie	Institute of Notre Dame, Baltimore	1996
Bevans, Kimberly	Chesapeake High School, Baltimore	1995
Carr, Holly	Delmar High School, Delmar	1995
Sowers, Dwight	Easton High School, Easton	1995
Hom, Ricky	Northern High School, Baltimore	1994
Witherspoon, Clarenth	Lake Clifton-Eastern High School, Baltimore	1993
(Mowers) Bohn, Adele	Francis Scott Key High School, Union Bridge	1992
Kennedy, Kristina	Northern High School, Ownings	1991
Gwathmey, Lisa	Suitland High School, District Heights	1990
Stone, Patrick	Jefferson City High School, Jefferson City	1989
Frank, Christopher	Centennial High School, Ellicott	1987

MASSACHUSETTS

Perfetuo, Kyla	Randolph High School, Randolph	1997
Santiago, Yiomara	Marlborough High School, Marlborough	1997
DeGirolamo, Robert	Foxborough High School, Foxborough	1996
Santos, Paula	Dennis-Yarmouth Regional High School, South Yarmouth	1996
Stone, Lisa	Amesbury High School, Amesbury	1995
White, Kathy	Hopkinton High School, Hopkinton	1995
Cascio, Beckie	Medway High School, Medway	1994
Sullivan, Erin	Quincy High School, Quincy	1994
MacDonald, Scott	Hanover High School, Hanover	1993
Behring, Annamarie	Chelmsford High School, Chelmsford	1992
Gelina, Laura	Marlboro High School, Marlboro	1991
Rogers, Cory	Middleboro High School, Middleboro	1990
McManus, Maura	Holbrook High School, Holbrook	1989

MICHIGAN

Barile, Annamaria	Thurston High School, Redford	1997
Yu, Nicholas	Lee M. Thurston High School, Redford	1997
Arsenault, Eric	L'Anse Creuse High School North, Macomb	1996
Golladay, Danette	Benton Harbor High School, Benton Harbor	1996
Thompson, Sarah	Lumen Christi High School, Jackson	1996
Ficklen, Cleven	Benton Harbor High School, Benton Harbor	1995
Gregones, Lisa	Northview High School, Grand Rapids	1995
Poszywak, Rachel	Pioneer High School, Ann Arbor	1995
DeClercq, Rob	Warren Woods Tower High School, Warren	1994
Johnson, LaKeyta	Benton Harbor High School, Benton Harbor	1994
Zelnik, Heather	Dondero High School, Royal Oak	1994
Bady, Annissa	Benton Harbor High School, Benton Harbor	1993
Jeffries, Antonia	Benton Harbor High School, Benton Harbor	1993
Williams, Armon	Creston High School, Grand Rapids	1993

Hamilton, Robin	Port Huron High School, Port Huron	1992
Shaw, Alden	Benton Harbor High School, Benton Harbor	1992
Garvin, Kentay	Pontiac Central High School, Pontiac	1991
Hutchinson, Kathleen	Benton Harbor High School, Benton Harbor	1990
White, Robert	Southaven High School, Southaven	1987

MINNESOTA

Shelquist, Nichole	Bagley High School, Bagley	1997
Zirbes, Brian	Melrose High School, Melrose	1997
Muenkel, Angela	Zumbrota/Mazeppa High School, Zumbrota	1996
Rowland, Vernon	De La Salle High School, Minneapolis	1996
Lehn, Jessi	Rothsay High School, Rothsay	1995
Stoner, Michael	Cathedral High School, St. Cloud	1995
Bautista, Mia	Chisholm High School, Chisholm	1994
Benedict, Priscilla	Pine River/Backus High School, Pine River	1994
Weeks, Amanda	Hermantown High School, Hermantown	1993
Kohanowski, Scott	Moorhead Senior High School, Moorhead	1992
Landkamer, Todd	Coon Rapids High School, Coon Rapids	1991
Warren, Desiree	North High School, Minneapolis	1990
Speer, Kellee	Eden Prairie High School, Eden Prairie	1989

MISSISSIPPI

Burton, Natalie	Pass Christian High School, Pass Christian	1997
Collins, Johnnie	Cathedral High School, Natchez	1997
Boykin, Thurman	Jackson Preparatory School, Jackson	1996
Shields, Stephanie	Starkville High School, Starkville	1996
Sexton, Tessa	Long Beach High School, Long Beach	1995
Smith, Billy	Lumberton High School, Lumberton	1995
Mapes, Chris	Biloxi High School, Biloxi	1994
Nash, Carrie	Pearl High School, Pearl	1993
Moorhead, Jasmine	Oxford High School, Oxford	1992
Staggs, Dana	MS School for Math & Science, Columbus	1991
Younce, Dallas	Jackson Preparatory High School, Jackson	1990
Barnes, Latesha	Bailey Alternative High School, Jackson	1988
Payne, Yolunda	Biloxi High School, Biloxi	1988
Burinskas, Matthew	Biloxi High School, Biloxi	1986
Pace, Jody	Pearl High School, Pearl	1986
O'Neal, Pamela	Southaven High School, Southaven	1985
Perry, Leslie	Jackson Preparatory School, Jackson	1985

MISSOURI

Kennedy, Nicole	Oak Park High School, Gladstone	1997
Patterson, Tenneille	Rolla High School, Rolla	1997
Lamp, Gregory	Trenton High School, Trenton	1996
Shafer, Steve	David H. Hickman High School, Columbia	1996
Shern, Brian	Belton High School, Belton	1995
Szucs, Kalman	Princeton High School, Princeton	1995
Cornell, Richard	Pattonville High School, Pattonville	1994
Meek, Tanimarrow	Smith-Cotton High School, Sedalia	1994
Dang, Adam	North Kansas City High School, North Kansas City	1993
Roth, Justin	Eureka Senior High School, Eureka	1992
Pope, Aaron	Rock Bridge Senior High School, Columbia	1991
Serig, Angela	Parkway Central High School, St. Louis	1990
Piepergerdes, Michael	North Kansas City High School, Kansas City	1988
Douthat, Trent	North Kansas City High School, North Kansas City	1985

MONTANA

Nadeau, Elizabeth	Hamilton High School, Hamilton	1997
Seitz, Mark	Darby High School, Darby	1997
Benjamin, Greta	Stevensville High School, Stevensville	1996
Thebo, Carrie Ann	Helena High School, Helena	1996
Holmes, Veronica	Great Falls High School, Great Falls	1995
Christensen, Jamie	Big Sky High School, Missoula	1994
Knudson, Kris	Highwood High School, Highwood	1993
Belcourt, Annjeanette	Browning High School, Browning	1992
Streber, Kay	Fergus High School, Lewistown	1991
Lester, Andrew	Stevensville High School, Stevensville	1990
Trueman, Shawn	Helena High School, Helena	1989

NEBRASKA

Baldwin, Celina	Oakland-Craig High School, Oakland	1997
Evans, Camekia	Burke High School, Omaha	1997
Lawson, Cassy	Millard South High School, Omaha	1996
Reineke, Kelly	Ord High School, Ord	1996
Blake, Amber	Hebron High School, Hebron	1995
Jahnke, Brandon	York High School, York	1995
Johnson, December	Bryan High School, Omaha	1994
Zessin, Amy	Gretna High School, Gretna	1993
Rediger, Wendy	Centennial Public School, Utica	1992
Summers, Monique	South High School, Omaha	1991
Nelms, Tracy	North Platte High School, North Platte	1990
Johnson, Don	Boys Town High School, Boys Town	1988
Cardenas, Anthony	Boys Town High School, Boys Town	1985
Oehring, Patricia	Lincoln Southeast High School, Lincoln	1985

NEVADA

Foster, Michael	Cimarron-Memorial High School, Las Vegas	1997
Marshall, Lindsay	Earl Wooster High School, Reno	1997
Hoopes, Heather	Chaparral High School, Las Vegas	1996
Cardona, Marylynn	Carlin High School, Carlin	1995
Wetzstein, Thomas	Incline High School, Incline Village	1994
Martinez, Neriza	Las Vegas High School, Las Vegas	1993
vanDrielen, Emily	McQueen High School, Reno	1992
Conrad, Tonya	Hug High School, Reno	1991
Leavitt, Guy	Sparks High School, Sparks	1990
Montes de Oca, April	Elko High School, Elko	1989

NEW HAMPSHIRE

Woodward, Benjamin	Newfound Regional High School, Bristol	1997
Hurd, William	Raymond High School, Raymond	1996
Beattie, Kelly	Timberlane Regional High School, Plaistow	1995
Gilman, Becky	Belmont High School, Belmont	1994

174

Roy, Isabelle	Manchester West High School, Manchester	1993
Duchesne, Amy	Berlin High School, Berlin	1992
Hagedorn, Kristen	Pelham High School, Pelham	1991
Perry, Douglas	Salem High School, Salem	1990

New Jersey

Flanagan, Vanessa	Kingsway Regional High School, Swedesboro	1997
Malkani, Amit	North Brunswick Township High School, North Brunswick	1997
Barron, Kathleen	North Hunterdon High School, Annandale	1996
Sokolowski, Brian	Steinert High School, Hamilton	1996
Sundell, Sarah	Delsea Regional High School, Franklinville	1995
Buchan, Meaghan	High Point Regional High School, Wantage	1994
Corcoran, Shannon	Ocean City High School, Ocean City	1994
Harris, Jes-Wá	N. Burlington Regional High School, Columbus	1993
Hogan, Brian	Boonton High School, Boonton	1992
Sinclair, Charles	Bayonne High School, Bayonne	1991
McKeaney, Anne	Holy Cross High School, Delran	1990
Martine, Lisa	Buena Regional High School, Buena	1988
Campbell, Colin	Red Bank Regional High School, Red Bank	1987
Van Brunt, Robert	Red Bank Regional High School, Little Silver	1985

New Mexico

Jimenez, Sarah	Rio Grande High School, Albuquerque	1997
Cruz, Phillip	Wagon Mound High School, Wagon Mound	1996
Vasquez, Angela	Taos High School, Taos	1995
Emillio, Lorenzo	San Jon High School, San Jon	1994
Wright, Willa	Gallup High School, Gallup	1993
Hankins, Linda	Ruidoso High School, Ruidoso	1992
Ontiveros, Artemio	Portales High School, Portales	1991
Padilla, Michael	Los Lunas High School, Los Lunas	1990
Martin, Phillip	Alamogordo High School, Alamogordo	1989

New York

Mullen, Kimberly	Martin Van Buren High School, Queens Village	1997
Zamor, Natacha	A. Philip Randolph Campus High School, New York	1997
Alvarado, Iris	Suffern High School, Suffern	1996
Rose, Daniell	Benjamin Cardozo High School, Jamaica	1996
Morris, Nora	Longwood Senior High School, Middle Island	1995
Soto, Jeannie	John Adams High School, Ozone Park	1995
Dinkes, Stephanie	Plainview-Old Bethpage JFK High School, Plainview	1994
Dunbar, Cheryl	August Martin High School, Jamaica	1994
Bryan, Jennifer	Williamsville East High School, East Amherst	1993
Sareen, Hema	Flushing High School, Flushing	1992
Fiore, Stewart	All Hallows High School, Bronx	1991
Solis, Claudia	Mother Cabrini High School, New York	1990

Kenefick, Katherine	Van Buren High School, Queens	1989
Kenefick, Kristine	Van Buren High School, Queens	1989
Fisher, Amy	Ramapo High School, Spring Valley	1988
Ma, Anh	Suffern High School, Suffern	1988
Bartkowiak, Anthony	Hutchinson Central Tech High School, Buffalo	1987
Weissman, Clifford	Jamaica High School, Jamaica	1987
Allen, Jeffrey	Springfield Gardens High School, Springfield Gardens	1986
Thompson, Ansell	The Dwight School, New York	1985

North Carolina

Allebach, Jennifer	Seventy-First High School, Fayetteville	1997
Hill, Yakhia	East Forsyth High School, Kernersville	1997
Williamson, Erin	E. A. Laney High School, Wilmington	1996
Zepeda, Eduardo	Douglas Byrd High School, Fayetteville	1996
Smith, Stacie	High Point Central High School, High Point	1995
Valdez, Andria	Pine Forest High School, Fayetteville	1995
Winn, April	Carver High School, Winston-Salem	1995
Winn, Kimberly	Carver High School, Winston-Salem	1995
Hines, Amy	Havelock High School, Havelock	1994
Marcello, Catherine	E. E. Smith High School, Fayetteville	1994
Rikard, Carlessia	Dudley High School, Greensboro	1994
Dunham, Therren	Westover High School, Fayetteville	1993
Minter, Douglas	John T. Hoggard High School, Wilmington	1993
Ash, Danielle	LeJeune High School, Camp LeJeune	1992
McMillian, Donelle	Byrd Senior High School, Fayetteville	1992
Moore, Rhonda	T. Wingate Andrews High School, High Point	1991
McLaurin, Rangel	E. E. Smith High School, Fayetteville	1990
McConnell, Sarah	Enloe High School, Raleigh	1989
Robinson, Tonya	Hillside High School, Durham	1988
Chadwick, Deborah	Durham High School, Durham	1987
Merritt, Lindsey	Hillside High School, Durham	1986
Cousar, Deborah	South Mecklenburg High School, Charlotte	1985
Bell, Sonya	Hillside High School, Durham	1984
Saunders, Pamela	Durham High School, Durham	1984

North Dakota

Brecht, David	Golden Valley High School, Golden Valley	1997
Engquist, Amber	Oakes High School, Oakes	1997
Glasser, Aric	Watford City High School, Watford City	1996
Skorick, Paul	Williston High School, Williston	1995
Vogel, Lynn	Bishop Ryan High School, Minot	1994
Gilliland, Grant	Beulah High School, Beulah	1993
Randa, Holly	Valley City High School, Valley City	1992
Knowlton, Tiffany	Grand Forks Central High School, Grand Forks	1991
Sagsveen, David	Century High School, Bismarck	1990
Osmundson, Patricia	Minot High School, Minot	1989

Ohio

Lowe, Gina	EHOVE Career Center, Milan	1997
Zickefoose, Bethany	Logan High School, Logan	1997
Jones, Joy	Whitmer High School, Toledo	1996
McClain, Shannon	Medina County Career Center, Medina	1996
Anastasio, Jennifer	Penta County Joint Vocational School, Perrysburg	1995

Tooley, Rachel	Wayne County Career Center, Smithville	1995
King, Tiffany	Portage Lakes Career Center, Greensburg	1994
Plescher, Gary	Ottawa-Glandorf High School, Ottawa	1994
Hahn, Margaret	Beavercreek High School, Beavercreek	1993
Ditchen, Tracie	Live Oaks C.D.C., Milford	1992
Moore, Holly	Six District Compact, Tallmadge	1991
Miller, Andrew	EHOVE Vocational School, Milan	1990
Lang, Stephanie	St. Ursula Academy, Cincinnati	1989
Coover, Christopher	Vandalia-Butler Senior High School, Vandalia	1988
Janselewitz, Steven	Rutherford B. Hayes High School, Delaware	1988
Stonerock, Bridgett	Kettering Fairmont High School, Kettering	1988
Gilp, Brian	Vandalia-Butler High School, Vandalia	1986
Shaw, Anne	St. Ursula Academy, Cincinnati	1986
Black, Paris	Columbus East High School, Columbus	1985
Gerhard, Susan	Kettering Fairmont High School, Kettering	1984

OKLAHOMA

Nelson, Brian	Westmoore High School, Oklahoma City	1997
Smith, Mariea	Valliant High School, Valliant	1997
Mason, Tommy	Laverne High School, Laverne	1996
Orrostieta, Vicki	Edmond Memorial High School, Edmond	1996
Hardesty, Stacy	Altus High School, Altus	1995
Wilson, Jamie	Jenks High School, Jenks	1995
Mericle, Christie	Chickasha High School, Chickasha	1994
Collins, Jennifer	Western Heights High School, Oklahoma City	1993
Hayes, Thomas	Union High School, Tulsa	1992
Rose, Mickey	Waurika High School, Waurika	1991
Wadsworth, Sheri	Sayre High School, Sayre	1990
Neese, Karla	Stillwater High School, Stillwater	1989
Sepeda, Staci	Stillwater High School, Stillwater	1987
Stahl, Michael	Putnam City North High School, Oklahoma City	1987
Pappas, Tina	Ponca City High School, Ponca City	1986
Heger, Lorie Ann	Putnam City North High School, Oklahoma City	1985

OREGON

Barrett, Bart	Cove High School, Cove	1997
Hubbard, Nicole	St. Mary's Academy for Girls, Portland	1997
Jeans-Gail, Katharine	St. Mary's Academy, Portland	1997
Smythe, Damon	Jesuit High School, Lake Oswego	1997
Thomas, Morgan	Bandon High School, Bandon	1997
Zimel, Gregory	Jesuit High School, Portland	1997
Gable, Tanya	Brookings-Harbor High School, Brookings	1996
Kerns, Heidi	North Powder High School, North Powder	1996
Edgel, Sally	Clackamus High School, Milwaukie	1995
Hubbard, Melissa	Union High School, Union	1995
Robertson, Lavert	Jefferson High School, Portland	1994
Scott, Chris	Ontario High School, Ontario	1993
Hatmaker, Jon	Henry D. Sheldon High School, Eugene	1992

Del Valle, Matthew	Nyssa High School, Nyssa	1991
Monteith, Trevor	Chiloquin High School, Chiloquin	1990
Glockler, Molly	Rogue River High School, Rogue River	1989
Howell, Kristin	Sunset High School, Beaverton	1989
Saunders, Cheryl	Phoenix High School, Phoenix	1988
Severson, Derek	South Medford High School, Medford	1987
Geiszler, Rodney	Phoenix High School, Phoenix	1986

PENNSYLVANIA

Jones, Kevin	Simon Gratz High School, Philadelphia	1997
Zermane, Erica	Wyoming Area High School, Exeter	1997
Lally, Michael	Interboro High School, Prospect Park	1996
Wilson, Kathryn	Central Cambria High School, Ebensburg	1996
Fenstermaker, Matthew	Northampton Area Sr. High School, Northampton	1995
Timmons, Tichianaa	Milton Hershey School, Hershey	1995
Kirchner, Fran	McCaskey High School, Lancaster	1994
Sinwell, Julia	John S. Brashear High School, Pittsburgh	1994
Morris, Wesley	Girard College, Philadelphia	1993
Magdich, Ed	Canon-McMillian Senior High School, Caninsburg	1992
Grove, Adam	William Penn High School, York	1991
Sheffield, Julie	North Penn High School, Lansdale	1990
Ferber, Cynthia	McDowell High School, Erie	1989
McFadden, Christopher	Allen High School, Allentown	1988
Yingst, David	Palmyra Area High School, Palmyra	1988
Cinfici, William	Reading Senior High School, Reading	1987

PUERTO RICO

Gonzalez, Ida	Luis Munoz Rivera High School, Utuado	1997
Martir, Osvaldo	Patria Latorre, San Sebastian	1997
Santana, Annelisse	Fernando Callejo, Manati	1996
Negron, Aixa	Luis Veronne High School, Canovanas	1995
Toro, Alba	Gautier Benitez High School, Caguas	1995
Rodriguez, Edwin	German Rieckehoff High School, Vieques	1994
Pagan, Francisco	D. A. Collazo High School, Lares	1993
Santiago Matos, Steven	Aguayo High School, Ponce	1992
Tapia, Luis	Carolina New Urban High School, Carolina	1991

RHODE ISLAND

Miller, Mendy	Scituate High School, North Scituate	1997
Saing, Aun	Mount Pleasant High School, Providence	1996
Pina, Carmen	Shea High School, Pawtucket	1995
Bugner, Stephen	North Providence High School, North Providence	1994
St. Jean, Julie	Smithfield High School, Smithfield	1993
Mei, Li Yu	East Greenwich High School, East Greenwich	1992
Bessette, Stephanie	Lincoln Jr.-Sr. High School, Lincoln	1991
Cherry, Michael	Warwick Veterans Memorial High School, Warwick	1990
Cantino, Tracey	Coventry High School, Coventry	1988

South Carolina

King, Richard	Cheraw High School, Cheraw	1997
Smith, Danny	Boiling Springs High School, Spartanburg	1997
Pugsley, Matthew	Paul M. Dorman High School, Spartanburg	1996
Church, Christine	Fort Mill High School, Fort Mill	1995
Cowans, Tishilia	Belton-Honea Path High School, Honea Path	1995
Lind, Russell	Riverside High School, Greer	1994
Oakley, Tara	Battery Creek High School, Burton	1993
Edmond, Dionne	W. J. Keenan High School, Columbia	1992
Smith, Barbara	Paul M. Dorman High School, Spartanburg	1991
Nixon, Richard	Richland Northeast High School, Columbia	1990
Cobbs, Catrele	Orangeburg-Wilkinson High School, Orangeburg	1988
Quay, Adam	Orangeburg-Wilkinson High School, Orangeburg	1986

South Dakota

Hedman, Alisha	T. F. Riggs High School, Pierre	1997
Ready, Benjamin	Bennett County School District, Martin	1997
Davidson, Shannon	Edgemont High School, Edgemont	1996
Olson, Ross	Madison High School, Madison	1995
Leinen, Jennifer	Lemmon High School, Lemmon	1994
Konechne, Dustin	Kimball High School, Kimball	1993
Behlings, Melissa	Millbank Sr. High School, Millbank	1992
Edwards, Michael	Belle Forche High School, Belle Forche	1991
Fast Horse, Michael	Lyman High School, Presho	1990

Tennessee

Hall, Mary	Pickett County High School, Byrdstown	1997
Owen, Melissa	Adamsville High School, Adamsville	1997
Boone, Ike	Whitehaven High School, Memphis	1996
Richardson, Michael	Fairview High School, Fairview	1996
King, Samantha	Oneida High School, Oneida	1995
Marcum, Melissa	Scott High School, Huntsville	1995
Johnson, Jennifer	Haywood High School, Brownsville	1994
Richardson, Michael	Powell High School, Powell	1994
Burrus, Amy	Dyersburg High School, Dyersburg	1993
Smith, Chad	Chester County High School, Henderson	1992
Cravens, Tonya	Alvin C. York Institute, Jamestown	1991
Lemke, Christine	Northwest High School, Clarkesville	1991
Nguyen, Ducphong	Craigmont High School, Memphis	1990
Yi, Bobby	Glencliff High School, Nashville	1989
Pruett, Judy	Bradley Central High School, Cleveland	1987

Texas

Evans, Erin	Robert E. Lee High School, Tyler	1997
Putnam, Misty	Arp High School, Arp	1997
Schroeder, Tanya	Brewer High School, Fort Worth	1996
Viasana, Rosa	Carthage High School, Carthage	1996
Banda, Armando	N. Garland High School, Garland	1995
McGee, Tiffany	Bishop T. K. Gorman High School, Tyler	1995
Gonzalez, Sandra	Georgetown High School, Georgetown	1994
Maxey, Sam	New Waverly High School, New Waverly	1994
Allbritton, Courtney	L. D. Bell High School, Hurst	1993
Guillory, Elizabeth	Monsignor Kelly High School, Beaumont	1993
Houdeshell, Seth	Taft High School, San Antonio	1992
Curl, Marquet	Nacogdoches High School, Nacogdoches	1991
Gunter, Traci	Paris High School, Paris	1990
Barreras, Amie	Martin High School, Arlington	1989
Reames, Julie	L. D. Bell High School, Hurst	1989
Fiore, Robert	Newman Smith High School, Carrollton	1988
Siemplenski, Janel	Marcus High School, Flower Mound	1988
Walker, Jason	Lamar Senior High School, Houston	1988
Cryer, Vance	L. D. Bell High School, Hurst	1987
Gotcher, Dusty	Grapevine High School, Grapevine	1987
Zamarripa, Robert	Harlingen High School, Harlingen	1987
Brown, Raquel	M. B. Lamar High School, Houston	1986
Painter, David	Trinity High School, Euless	1986
Boyter, Michael	L. D. Bell High School, Hurst	1985
Brown, Lisa	Grapevine High School, Grapevine	1985
White, Christina	Odessa High School, Odessa	1985
Brooks, Ray	Grapevine High School, Grapevine	1984
Cameron, Jayna	L. D. Bell High School, Hurst	1984

Utah

Nielson, Christian	Sky View High School, Smithfield	1997
Smith, Maren	Logan High School, Logan	1996
Swain, Colette	Pine View High School, St. George	1995
Sepulveda, Alejandro	Alta High School, Sandy	1994
Baustert, Heather	Layton High School, Layton	1993
Muavesi, Ita	Hillcrest High School, Midvale	1992
Jensen, Christine	Ogden High School, Ogden	1991
Jackson, Collin	Whitehorse High School, Montezuma Creek	1990
Harward, Jennifer	Davis High School, Kaysville	1989

Vermont

Dion, Joshua	Twinfield Union High School, Plainfield	1997
Godfrey, Tracy	Montpelier High School, Montpelier	1997
Hall, Adam	South Burlington High School, South Burlington	1996
Rogers, Jaime	Champlain Valley Union High School, Hinesburg	1995
Choma, Joe	Otter Valley Union High School, Sudbury	1994
Preston, Ann	Colchester High School, Colchester	1993
Rowell, Shauna	Cabot School, Cabot	1992
Chalue, Jeanine	Hozen Union High School, Hardwick	1991
Mitchell, Hannah	Montpelier High School, Montpelier	1990

Virgin Islands

Smith, Raynise	Ivanna Eudora Kean High School, Charlotte Amalie	1993
Sanchez-Morales, Elisamuel	Charlotte Amalie High School, St. Thomas	1992
Dowell, Dorsity	St. Croix Central High School, Christiansted	1991

VIRGINIA

Lloyd, Aisha	Martinsville High School, Martinsville	1997
Terry, Tonisha	John F. Kennedy High School, Richmond	1997
Johnson, Randy	Nelson County High School, Lovingston	1996
Young, Audrey	Courtland High School, Spotsylvania	1996
Sinnett, Tracey	Turner Ashby High School, Bridgewater	1995
Cowan, Allen	Buckingham County High School, Buckingham	1994
Flanagan, Maria	Magna Vista High School, Ridgeway	1994
Webber, Jennifer	Patrick Henry High School, Roanoke	1993
Foltz, Jennifer	Appomattox County High School, Appomattox	1992
Feliu, Josep	Quantico High School, Quantico	1991
Thomas, Tracy	Gar-Field High School, Dale City	1991
Hutcherson, Andrea	Mills Godwin High School, Richmond	1990
Mawler, Lea Ann	Berryville High School, Berryville	1990
Rawlings, Kevin	John F. Kennedy High School, Richmond	1988

WASHINGTON

Kloepper, Le An	Nooksack Valley High School, Everson	1997
Page, Michael	Connell High School, Connell	1997
Forrest, Mandee	Selah High School, Selah	1996
Przybylski, Heather	Liberty High School, Renton	1996
Sherrod, Nathaniel	Walla Walla High School, Walla Walla	1995
Smith, Jason	Cashmere High School, Cashmere	1995
Bicknell, Justin	Sedro-Woolley High School, Sedro-Woolley	1994
Espindola, Manuel	La Conner High School, La Conner	1994
Gillison, Joy	Peninsula High School, Gig Harbor	1993
Pham, By	A. C. Davis High School, Yakima	1992
Schultz, Kenneth	Pasco Senior High School, Pasco	1991
Glenn, Anita	Shelton High School, Shelton	1990
Clark, Amanda	Centralia High School, Centralia	1985

WEST VIRGINIA

Smith, Hanna	Pocahontas County High School, Dunmore	1997
Stitzel, James	Tygarts Valley High School, Mill Creek	1997
Hileman, Christie	Doddridge County High School, West Union	1996
Chenoweth, Rebecca	Elkins High School, Elkins	1995
Pecora, Angela	Martinsburg High School, Martinsburg	1994
Stevenson, Sonynita	Preston High School, Kingwood	1993
Livesay, Steven	Clay County High School, Clay	1992
Truluck, Norma	Capital High School, Charleston	1991
Conkle, Laura	Oak Glen High School, New Cumberland	1990
James, Lee	Brooke High School, Wellsburg	1989

WISCONSIN

Hernandez, Christopher	Waukesha North High School, Waukesha	1997
McDaniel, Antonio	Milwaukee Bay View High School, Milwaukee	1997
Hollister, Mary	Mondovi High School, Mondovi	1996
Rud, Dana	Parker High School, Janesville	1996
Denke, Tanya	Antigo High School, Deerbrook	1995
Nuutinen, Tara	Mellen High School, Mellen	1995
Eggebrecht, Rachel	Merrill Senior High School, Merrill	1994
Zopp, Amanda	Hayward High School, Hayward	1994
Huang, Michael	Eau Claire Memorial High School, Eau Claire	1993
Davis, Ann	Wausau East High School, Wausau	1992
Ferge, Peter	Horicon High School, Horicon	1991
Maus, Jodi	Rice Lake High School, Rice Lake	1990
Toft, Mark	Rice Lake High School, Rice Lake	1990
Nalker, Denise	Bradford High School, Kenosha	1989
Jones, Julie	Pius XI High School, Milwaukee	1984

WYOMING

Hansen, Alicia	Kemmerer High School, Kemmerer	1997
Kruse, James	Niobrara High School, Lusk	1997
Mauch, Karl	Pinedale High School, Pinedale	1996
Van Alyne, Robert	Cheyenne Central High School, Cheyenne	1995
Sandy, Ben	New Castle High School, New Castle	1994
Hacklin, Deena	Big Piney High School, Big Piney	1993
Karhu, Karna	Riverside High School, Basin	1992
Jones, Lola	Hot Spring County High School, Thermopolis	1991
Farmer, Brenda	Natrona County High School, Casper	1990

HORATIO ALGER ASSOCIATION

Terrence J. Giroux, Executive Director
Biographies by Jackie Rough